STORIES
FROM THE
SHELTER

"If you want to understand the inside story of homelessness, *Stories from the Shelter* is essential reading. Barrow reveals in living color the unvarnished realities of life on the street and the inspiring (and often disappointing) efforts to ignite hope in the spirits of broken people."

—DR. ROBERT LUPTON,
author of *Compassion, Justice, and the Christian Life* and *Toxic Charity*

Blake Barrow is a fantastic storyteller and a genuinely good and passionate man. His stories will touch your heart as he describes what it takes to confront homelessness each day.

—REV. ANDY BALES,
CEO, Union Rescue Mission,
Los Angeles, California

The names change, the places are different, but all of us who work in rescue missions recognize the stories. They are filled with emotion and conflict. We have seen people who embrace a new life in Christ and do very well, and then we are frustrated by those we just can't reach. This book tells the reality of both experiences.

—RICK ALVIS,
CEO, Wheeler Mission Ministries,
Indianapolis, IN

With a lawyer's attention to detail, Blake Barrow finds creative solutions to hurting peoples' problems while effectively sharing his faith in all conditions and circumstances.

—DAVID TREADWELL,
Executive Director, Central Union Mission,
Washington, DC

STORIES
FROM THE
SHELTER

A Lawyer's Ministry with God's
Children who are Homeless

BLAKE W. BARROW

WESTBOW°
PRESS
A DIVISION OF THOMAS NELSON
& ZONDERVAN

WestBow Press books may be ordered through booksellers or by contacting:

WestBow Press
A Division of Thomas Nelson & Zondervan
1663 Liberty Drive
Bloomington, IN 47403
www.westbowpress.com
1 (866) 928-1240

Because of the dynamic nature of the Internet, any web addresses or
links contained in this book may have changed since publication and
may no longer be valid. The views expressed in this work are solely those
of the author and do not necessarily reflect the views of the publisher,
and the publisher hereby disclaims any responsibility for them.

Any people depicted in stock imagery provided by Thinkstock are models,
and such images are being used for illustrative purposes only.
Certain stock imagery © Thinkstock.

ISBN: 978-1-4908-2519-9 (sc)
ISBN: 978-1-4908-2520-5 (hc)
ISBN: 978-1-4908-2518-2 (e)

Library of Congress Control Number: 2014905053

Printed in the United States of America.

WestBow Press rev. date: 06/30/2014

This book is dedicated to the long-term staff of the Rescue Mission of El Paso who, although materially underpaid, have continually and joyfully proclaimed the great love of Jesus to those who are homeless, thereby acquiring great spiritual wealth.

Staff members with at least 5 years of service	Years
Juana Ortega	26
Harvey Sharpe	17
Julius Martin	17
Blake W. Barrow	16
Bill Cox	14
George Sigales	13
Darlene Domingue	12
Diego Ochoa	11
Sam Casper	9
Florence Fowler	8
Stan Sanchez	6
Hal Tucker	5

All royalties from the sales of this book shall be used to advance God's ministry at the Rescue Mission of El Paso.

The first printing of this book has been made possible by the generous contributions from the following:

Casa Ford & Casa Nissan

Ray, McChristian & Jeans

Jordan Foster Construction

Hoy Fox Automotive Group

Marlene and J. O. Stewart Foundation

El Paso area Jack-in-the-Box Restaurants

CONTENTS

PREFACE

I LOVE GOING ON SPEAKING engagements to tell people about the great work that God is doing at the Rescue Mission of El Paso. If it is an informal setting such as a Rotary Club meeting or a Sunday school class, there is always time to take questions from the audience. I don't know if I consistently fail to explain things very well the first time, or if I get the people so interested in the work of the Mission that they always want to know more, but inevitably, I get lots of questions.

After several years of speaking to groups of people and fielding their questions, I have found myself repeating the same words. I would listen to the question, think a few seconds, and then say, "That reminds me of a story…," and I would answer their question with a short story of a real-life encounter from working with people who are homeless at the Mission.

Some of the stories make me laugh and some make me cry. Some have hit me on such a personal level that I cannot talk about them at all without getting choked up. Fortunately, I am able to write about them without crying over the keyboard and shorting it out.

Several years ago I met Daniel Tovar at the Mission. He had a Ph.D. in sociology and had been working as a university professor in Oregon. We never discussed the details of how he lost his teaching position, but I presumed alcoholism played some role. Of course, jobs for sociology professors don't open up very often. When Daniel heard that the University of Texas at El Paso had an opening, he hitched several rides and made his way to El Paso.

The Rescue Mission is on the south side of Interstate 10, only a thousand yards or so from the university on the north side of I-10. Daniel came into the Mission hoping to get cleaned up and find some better clothes before going for his interview.

Once I met Daniel, I was excited about the opportunity of helping him succeed. I took him to Men's Warehouse for a custom-fitted suit and then to my barber. After a few hours of work, he looked like he was ready to conquer the world.

Daniel went for his interview and was really pumped up about his chances of getting in. Two weeks later, however, he heard that UTEP had hired someone else for the position. Daniel fell back into depression, and his alcoholism took over.

For the next few months, he was in and out of the Rescue Mission. He would sober up for a while and come in for some good food, a shower, and a bed, and then relapse to the streets for another extended drunk.

At one point after he had been away from the bottle long enough to be thinking clearly, I presented him with an idea.

"Daniel, you have now been hanging around the Rescue Mission for over six months. How many books are there which accurately describe homelessness in America?"

I could see the wheels starting to turn in his brain as he paused for about ten seconds.

"There aren't any!" He seemed shocked by the sudden revelation.

"Exactly," I said, "I thought so. You are the perfect person to write it, and I will help you."

Daniel seemed excited about his new-found purpose. I gave him a pad and pen for him to start writing down thoughts, but within a week Daniel disappeared again, and I knew that our joint excitement had been drowned in a bottle somewhere.

The pattern continued. Daniel would sober up and come into the Mission for help, but then, within another ten days, he was gone again.

After a few cycles, I got a call from a social worker at Thomason Hospital. Daniel was about to be discharged and they wanted to be sure we had space for him at the Mission. He had fallen into the irrigation canal, broken his ankle, and almost drowned. Some Border Patrol agents were able to fish him out of the water and revive him, but no one knew how long he had been under.

The experience motivated him for several months of sobriety, but it also cost him dearly. I could tell that his brain was no longer functioning the way it had before, and I knew that Daniel was now incapable of completing our project.

About two years later, I presided over Daniel's funeral. He got drunk, stepped out onto a busy street in the dark, and was run over so many times that his head separated from the rest of his body.

I never forgot "our" project.

If you ask me who are the people who are homeless in America, I will have trouble answering the question. All of them are unique with unique sets of problems and circumstances that have contributed to their becoming homeless. Consequently, no one program or solution is effective for every individual.

To use the forest and the trees line, I can describe this tree, and this tree, and this tree, and after about forty trees, you will have a very good idea of what the forest looks like.

This book is Daniel's project to answer the question of who are these people who are homeless in America—or, at least, who are the homeless people who have come through the Rescue Mission of El Paso?

The question I have been asked most often at my speaking engagements is, "How did you go from being a trial lawyer to running a homeless shelter?" The first chapter tells that story.

Chapter 2 is my initiation into Christian ministry in the shelter setting. Then the book dives into a series of chapters which describe each tree. If you want to read about the people who are homeless and are not interested in reading about who is telling the stories, just skip to the third chapter.

The last chapter is an epilogue written by Taylor Hernandez, a high school student who came to volunteer at the Rescue Mission. She came to fulfill her community service requirements for the honor society, and she had so much fun volunteering one summer that she kept coming back for more. After I have described many trees, you then get to read about some of those same trees as seen through another set of eyes.

While this preface is probably the first part of this book that you are reading, it is one of the last sections that I wrote. I have heard from many authors about their starting to write on one particular theme, and as they are writing, something else came out. I started out trying to personalize the people who are homeless in the same manner that I would start a trial by introducing my client to the jury. The secondary theme that emerged as I was writing is the story of how God has led me in this ministry for which I did not go to school, was never trained, and frequently feel like I don't have a clue what I am doing. I never expected to find myself running a shelter. I was trained to present lawsuits to juries. However, I know how to pray and listen, and when God called, I did not run away. Then, once I had taken the steps to do the things that God told me to do, God showed up to finish the work with the result that the Rescue Mission has become a divine tool to meet the needs of thousands of people in extreme poverty while transforming their lives through the Gospel.

In the same manner that God has used a lawyer to proclaim the Gospel to the poor, God can use anyone who is willing to pray and listen and submit to God's calling.

I will be the first to tell you that I still do not know everything about how to run a Rescue Mission. Moses protested that he could not speak well and was not the person to approach Pharaoh. There is a lesson here that God is able to use us in the areas where we think we are the weakest, if we allow God to work through us.

As I now look back upon all of the events in my life, I can recognize that each experience, each college degree, each job, was God preparing me for the highest calling imaginable—proclaiming the Gospel of Jesus Christ to the poor. Sometimes I use my mouth, but most of my preaching is with my hands.

CHAPTER 1

THE CALL

I WAS SITTING AT MY desk working when God called. I had just finished the biggest case of my career and was trying to catch up on the other cases which had been pushed to the back of the file cabinet. The case came in the office in February, and from that time until the August trial, it took 90% of my time.

I had a theory that one lawyer could effectively manage about 50 cases. If the lawyer had a good paralegal, that number could grow to 75. With two good paralegals, maybe 100 to 125 cases were manageable. I had tried a few paralegals with poor results and was working by myself with about 85 cases. I was buried with work.

My largest client was a trucking company based in Cedar Rapids, Iowa. It ran about 800 tractor-trailers across the United States and gave me all of its personal injury litigation cases west of the Mississippi. That geographic restriction was mine.

The work had begun when one of their trucks had an accident

in El Paso and was sued here. Since my favorite private investigator did work for the trucking company, he recommended me to defend its case in El Paso. The case went all the way through a jury trial and resulted in a "take nothing" verdict for the defendant trucking company. After the case was over, I added up my hours and out-of-pocket expenses. I was a solo practitioner, and my largest category of overhead was the salary of the receptionist, which I split with another lawyer who occupied the office next to mine. Rent was $350. The next largest expense was the copy machine at $50 per month. I was a lean, mean, lawyerly machine. I multiplied my hours by $75 and added in the costs of hiring a consulting engineer and all travel expenses. The final bill came to a hair over $10,000. I wrote up a complete bill and put it in the mail.

Three days later, I got a phone call from the loss control manager at the trucking company. I was thinking, "OK, here we go again, she is calling to complain about my bill."

Instead, the conversation went like this:

"I got your bill in the mail."

"Yes."

"Is this your final bill?"

"Well, of course. The case is over."

A long pause.

"Do you do work outside of El Paso?"

"I suppose I could, but I have enough work to keep me busy right here."

"If I send you some cases from other cities, will you do them?"

"Well, I will look at them. But if I have to go out of town, I'll need to increase my hourly rate a bit."

"Fine."

Within a week I had two cases in Houston, one in San Antonio and one in Dallas. Since all of the cases had been removed to federal court on diversity jurisdiction, it was no big deal. All of the rules were the same. I could appear in federal court in Houston and be just as comfortable as I was in federal court in El Paso.

When I started reading through the files coming from Houston, I completely understood where the trucking company was coming from. Some of the former law firms included copies of their invoices with the files containing the pleadings and discovery. I saw very quickly that I could get on Southwest Airlines and cover the court hearings in Houston for less than the lawyers from the big Houston firms were charging to walk across the street. While I knew that my bills were on the low end of the lawyerly spectrum, I could not have imagined where the high end was until I saw their invoices. They were charging five times my fee. Furthermore, since a plane trip to Houston meant an opportunity to go visit my parents and stay with them, I did not have to charge for a hotel stay.

The system worked so well that within a few weeks I was receiving cases from Nevada and California. When a case came in from Trenton, New Jersey, I felt the need to protest. I called the trucking company and explained that a lawyer needs to be able to relate to and understand the mind-set of the jury. I thought it was a stretch to ask a west Texas lawyer to relate to a jury in New Jersey. I made some calls to find an affordable New Jersey lawyer and passed that one on. Thankfully, the company accepted my recommendation, and we agreed that I would be responsible only for those cases west of the Mississippi.

In addition to the work from the trucking company, I had dozens of cases right here in El Paso. I never had a Yellow Pages ad larger than a business card, but I was flooded with work. For the longest time I refused to accept divorce cases. When people came into my office asking about a divorce, I would open my Rolodex to the entry on marriage counselors and give them some recommendations. Instead of referring to Texas law, I advised them how God's plan was for a man and a woman to become one person in the sight of God. I talked about the differences between a contract and a covenant.

Usually the people just stared at me with a look that said, "I sure am glad I didn't pay for this 'legal' consultation." After about fifty of these rejected cases, the revelation started to sink in to me that by the time the people came to a lawyer's office to start the process of a divorce, the marriage was dead. At that point, the best thing that could be done was to bury what was dead and allow the people to start over. Through much prayer, I believe God was telling me that I had the capacity to process a divorce economically and expediently, and that if I refused to do so, the people would simply go down the street to the atheist divorce lawyer who would be pleased to pursue their divorce and take all their money in the process. In the end, they would still be divorced, but now they would hate the other spouse forever for having been dragged through the awful legal process. If I attempted the divorce in a peaceful manner, at least the possibility of eventual reconciliation was still there.

Again, I started out too economically and, as a result, was flooded with more work. I charged $500 for a simple divorce and $500 plus the filing fee if there were children involved. Once I had typed all of the forms into the computer, all I had to do was change the names and press the "print" button. I used one form if the petitioner was the wife and another form if the husband was the petitioner, so I didn't even need to change "he" to "she" wherever it appeared. I could still make close to $100 per hour on most cases.

Amazingly, it was in the process of handling divorce cases that I came to a greater understanding of how to trust God. Out of the hundreds of divorce cases that I processed, I had maybe two or three people who paid me with a check. All the rest paid with cash, and it was almost always with $100 bills. I would take the money, record it in my accounting ledger, and put the bills in my pocket. I spent a few of them, but when Sunday came, if there were any of those

$100 divorce bills in my wallet, I pulled them out and put them into the offering plate. I seldom even filled out the offering envelope that was in the church pews. I didn't care about the tax receipt. I still considered it dirty money and just wanted to get rid of it.

Running a litigation practice, I usually got paid when a case was concluded. If it was a plaintiff's case on a contingency fee, I didn't get paid at all if I didn't win. There were many weeks when the receptionist made more money than I did. Sometimes I went for three or four weeks without earning anything at all. But my wife still reminded me about the mortgage payments, the car payments, and expenses for the kids.

It didn't take too many Sundays of throwing that dirty money into the plate until I began to spot a trend. If I started the week by making an extra financial contribution to God's work, then God's blessings were sure to follow. Usually the time lag was only a few days. Maybe I had a long-ignored legal case which was just sitting on the shelf. I had not done anything to stimulate activity, but the insurance adjuster would call and say, "I need to get this file off of my desk. I am increasing my settlement offer by $5,000. Can we resolve this claim?" The case in which I least expected a quick resolution would settle out, and I had unexpected income.

I began to spot a very clear pattern of "if-then" relationships of events. If I take this filthy, sin-stained $100 bill and throw it in the offering plate, then God's blessings will follow.

After a while, I began to bank on the experience. If I had some bills coming due, I would deposit the dirty dollars in the plate and then wait to see how God would return the investment—call it theological money laundering. If I had to come up with several thousand dollars to pay taxes in a few weeks, I should not hoard those dirty $100 bills so that I could use them to pay the taxes. I should give them to God, and God would return a far greater amount of clean money. The more time that passed, the more comfortable I was trusting God. I learned that as long as I was living in God's will, then God would supply all of my needs. The amount of money I was making on my own was irrelevant. I was rubbing shoulders with many lawyers who were making a lot more money than I was, and most of them were miserable.

Along with trusting God more came spending more time with God in prayer. I probably spent more time in prayer than I did doing legal research. I began each research session with, "Lord God, show me where to find the answers to these legal questions." Then I listened for God's voice before proceeding. I did the same thing when a new case came into the office. "Jesus, do you want me to take this case?" Before long about one-third of my legal case load was being done *pro bono* for the poor, yet my income was actually higher.

Of course, the issue of learning that I could trust God is probably better phrased in reverse. I was spending more time in prayer and giving a greater percentage of the blessings God had provided back to God's work, so I was becoming more trustworthy to God. As God saw that I was not going to hoard the money or spend it on myself for things I really didn't need, then God began to provide more knowing that I could be trusted to use it to advance God's purposes.

Another side of the spiritual laws that I was learning in my human law practice was that when things were not going very well, I could not improve them by working harder. Instead, I needed to spend more time in prayer and reexamine my activities to be sure that I was working where God wanted me to work. If my work was not being blessed, then perhaps I had missed God's direction and was off working on my own. My task then became more of a challenge to discern what God was doing and then to put myself in the middle of it.

Now that I had learned these lessons, the voice of God came to me from a most unexpected source.

I was renting my corner office from James Carroll, another

lawyer who had leased the entire top floor of the building. He had aspirations of creating the premier labor law firm in El Paso, so he leased a huge space and was occupying about 30% of it. He wanted to fill the remainder with his associates, but that dream had not yet materialized. So to help with the lease payments, he sublet a large corner office to me.

About 6:30 one evening after everyone else had gone home, James walked into my office. My corner was the last stop before the elevator, so it was not unusual for him to stick his head in and wave goodnight. This visit was different, though. He came in and plopped down in the chair in front of my desk and started complaining about how unreasonable the Board was at the Rescue Mission. James had told me about the Mission months before, and I knew that he was the president-elect of the Board of the Mission. I had lived in El Paso for almost ten years, and I vaguely knew of its existence but not much more. Following his introduction, I got a call from the Mission's Executive Director and scheduled a lunch meeting at the Mission. On the appointed day I took a tour of the building and sat down with the Director for a really excellent lunch. I returned to my office and wrote a $1000 contribution check to the Rescue Mission and put it in the mail. The lunch, a 30 minute tour, and my one contribution were the extent of my involvement with, or knowledge of, the Rescue Mission of El Paso.

James proceeded to tell me how the Executive Director had made a mess of things and that the Board had finally fired him. Then the Board brainstormed attributes they wanted in the next Director. He kept saying over and over, "They're nuts, they're nuts, they will never find anyone to do this job." I didn't put it together at the time, but I think his real fear was that he, as the next president of the Board, would wind up running the Mission which would greatly interfere with the time he spent in his labor law practice.

He then plowed into all of the Board's expectations: "They want a family man who is here in El Paso, who is active in a major church, who has run his own business, who has some legal background, who has a seminary degree...." James kept listing off at least ten other attributes and each one hit me like a dart in the head. My mother could not have described my life experiences so accurately.

I had four degrees including a Master of Theological Studies from Emory University before I went to Baylor Law School. Every single attribute that James mentioned fit me. I thought, "There are 600,000 people in El Paso and how many would fit this profile?"

"One."

"OK, God. This is really creepy. What are you trying to tell me?"

James kept on talking to himself, but I wasn't really listening any longer. I was praying and listening to God. The voice of God was as clear as I had ever heard it.

"Why don't you quit suing people and do something productive for the Kingdom of God?"

"Wow, you wouldn't want to sugar-coat that a bit would you God?"

No response.

Just silence.

Of course, James was still talking, but I didn't hear him.

"OK. I will do it."

The time that had passed since I started praying was about 30 seconds. But I knew with a certainty that I had heard from God. It wouldn't do any good to argue.

After some more prayer time, I realized that I had invited this dramatic change in my vocation. At one time my law office was just three blocks from St. Clement's Church. The Church held luncheons for local missionaries on the first Monday of every month. Since the Church advertised the meetings to be open to all of its members in addition to the missionaries, I started going. I met people there who had not only confessed Jesus as their savior but had done far more.

All of their labor each day was spent in building up the Kingdom of God. It took different forms. Some of them were caring for poor children in Mexico, others would take the Gospel to prisoners at the jail, and others reached out to troubled kids or helped people on drugs find freedom in Jesus.

We often hear people talk about giving their lives to Christ. We say it so casually. However, if we have really given our lives to Christ, it seems there should be a huge change in the way we are living, including the thousands of hours we spend at work. I believe there must be a big difference between accepting Jesus as your savior and giving your life to Christ. If I have given my life to Christ, then I don't own it or control it any more. When I go to work, am I doing something for Jesus, or better said, is Jesus doing something through me? Am I building up the Kingdom of God, or am I just trying to cash out the next legal case? Certainly, I was standing up for people's legal rights, but how many of those legal rights translated into eternal values? I remembered Jesus' response to the request of "make my brother share the inheritance with me."

I had met Alex Blomerth in church, but I got to know him at the missionary lunches. Alex would preside over the meetings, and he would move from table to table and call on individuals at the table to stand up and tell the group how God was moving in their particular ministry. Alex knew I was working as a lawyer, but he didn't skip over me when my turn came. I had to stand up and tell the group how God was moving in my work. So I told them I had a ministry of law and tried to relate some case that I was working on to a divine purpose.

As a lawyer I was accustomed to looking the jury straight in the eye and telling them the best story I could which had some support in the evidence. Whether or not I believed the story myself was really irrelevant. I just didn't expect to find myself having to draw on those same lawyerly skills at the missionary lunch.

I began to pray, "God, is there a real ministry that I can do?" "Can you put a lawyer to productive use for the Kingdom of God?" "If you have anything for me, here I am."

I later discovered that Alex Blomerth was praying the same prayer for me.

I do not think God forgets prayers like that. I wonder what happens in the spiritual realms when someone prays such a prayer. I imagine God blew his big whistle and ordered all his best angels to the conference table. "Now, we need to start cleaning Blake up a bit if he is going to be any use to us." The commands started flying, angels took their orders, and everyone got to work.

In my case it took God and a whole fleet of angels about eighteen months of cleaning time between mission lunch and mission calling.

In retrospect, I made one very big mistake in answering God's call. While my faith had grown sufficiently for me to trust God and to identify God's voice, my faith had not yet grown enough to allow me to keep other areas of my life in order. When I was sure that I had heard God's voice, I jumped in response without thinking through all of the consequences. For years I had turned divorce clients away with God's counsel that "the two shall become one flesh," even though I was still struggling to figure out just how such a spiritual mystery occurred.

A wise man would have said, "James, you are giving me some very interesting thoughts. Let me pray about these things, and I need to discuss them with my wife." I was not that wise.

In fact, even though I knew I had heard the voice of God, I was still thinking only of myself and God's call to use me. I had forgotten that "me" has another part. More disturbingly, although it took me several more years to admit it, I did not have enough faith to believe that God could speak to my wife just like God had spoken to me. By jumping in and making the decision without even consulting her, I deprived God of the opportunity to have that conversation with her. I was being an impediment to my wife's spiritual growth. Perhaps I was willing to act on God's call in areas of my life where I had complete control, but I did not have enough faith to believe that God could move others to respond as I had done.

As Christian men we are taught to take the leadership role in our families, but far too little discussion goes on as to appropriate leadership styles. Joseph Stalin's style is probably not a good one to emulate.

The next day James came back to see me, and we discussed a few of the details of my new calling including the amount of money the Board had authorized for a salary. The amount was one-third of what I had made the previous year as a lawyer, but I had learned the lesson that if you are in the will of God, then God will supply all of your needs without regard to your income. So I told James the salary was fine, and I still had not consulted my wife.

In fact, it took several more days before I worked up the nerve to dictate to her what I was going to do.

Sixteen years have passed. I cannot imagine a more fulfilling job than reaching out to the poorest of the poor with the love of Jesus. I don't have as much money as I used to, but I have no need for the money. God has provided for all of my needs. Best of all, my wife started to speak to me again after a few years, and she still reminds me what great eternal rewards she will have for putting up with me. I do not doubt she is correct.

Chapter 2

First Sermon

ONCE I HAD COMMITTED TO signing on at the Rescue Mission, my thoughts turned to the days on the calendar. Thanksgiving was approaching, and I figured that day was a really big deal for the Mission. I told James Carroll that I needed to be at the Mission long enough before Thanksgiving to have some idea what was up. James agreed; we met with the Board, and my hire date was set for November 10, 1997.

Two and one-half weeks was just barely enough time to grasp much of what was going on at the Mission. As I expected, Thanksgiving was a really big deal. Not only did we treat our own residents to a great feast, but also we fed hundreds of people from the community who might not be able to afford a full Thanksgiving meal. Our guests started lining up around 10:00 a.m. I observed that our chaplain was the key figure in the entire process. He explained the routine. As the people arrived, they were greeted and ushered into the chapel for a service. Then we dismissed them into the dining room and received the next wave of guests into the chapel. The cycle continued until all had heard the Gospel and all were fed. For the typical Thanksgiving Day, processing all of the visitors and guests could take three to four chapel services.

Our chaplain at that time was Pappy Hoyle. I loved Pappy. He had been instrumental, along with James, in introducing me to the work of the Rescue Mission. Pappy had been preaching at the Mission for at least the previous 20 years. He had been a motorcycle sergeant with the El Paso Police Department. Of course, most of the policemen on motorcycle patrol were much younger, and Pappy was in his 60s when he was still going strong with the motorcycle crew—hence the name "Pappy." He loved the Mission, and he loved the people the Mission served, and I loved him for it. He was a little rough on the edges and very direct—just as you would expect from a retired motorcycle police sergeant. I can just picture him riding his police motorcycle over to the Mission at the end of his shift and marching through the Mission in his police uniform commanding residents to appear in the chapel for his evening service. I am sure each session was full.

I actually met Pappy through James. Pappy had a personal injury law case, and he had asked James to represent him. But since James did only labor law, he referred Pappy's personal injury claim to me. It didn't take too many hours of working on Pappy's case until I knew volumes about the Rescue Mission and its ministry—at least from Pappy's perspective.

As more people came into the Mission, I quickly observed that one of Pappy's greatest challenges of the day was to be sure that no one went directly into the dining room without coming into the chapel first. The service consisted of a hymn, a 20-minute message to remind us that everything we had to be thankful for was a gift from God, an altar call, a final hymn, and dismissal into the dining room for the feast. I noticed that the service was shorter than Pappy's typical one—probably because he wanted to open up the doors for the next wave of hungry souls. During the last hymn, Pappy moved to the back of the chapel so he could shake hands with all the guests before they moved into the dining room which was directly across the hall from the rear chapel door. I was seated up front, so he grabbed me by the arm and pulled me along on his way to the rear of the chapel while giving me instructions that I was to join him in greeting all of the guests on their way out.

I thought it was a great service. The audience was a mixture of outside visitors and guests who were staying at the Mission, so there were many new faces in the crowd. Everyone seemed very pleased to be there and very grateful for the food they were about to receive.

Pappy had been holding his big, black, leather-bound Bible in his left hand while shaking hands with his right. If the dictionary had a listing for "old-school, country Baptist," I would expect to find Pappy's picture there.

Just as the last of our guests had exited the chapel to the dining room, Pappy moved his big Bible into his right hand and swung his arm around to me, slapping the big Bible into my belly with a thud that almost took my breath away. "Here," he proclaimed, "You take the next one."

It was a hand-off that any football coach would have been proud of. The most important factor is to avoid a fumble with the exchange, so the quarterback takes the ball and plants it so firmly in the running back's gut that the natural reaction is to wrap both arms instantly around it.

I didn't drop the Bible. Of course, it was more than a physical hand-off. It was a spiritual test. A response of, "Uh, well, I haven't really had time to prepare a message," would not do. It was the tough, old motorcycle sergeant's statement to the young kid, "I have spent a good portion of my life preaching to people who are homeless. You think you can follow in my footsteps? Let's see what you've got."

My mind raced back to the last time I had delivered a sermon in a church. It was youth Sunday, and I was the youth director at St. John's United Methodist Church in Rockdale, Texas, in my senior year in college. That was in 1979—eighteen years before. I did deliver a short sermon in my Professional Assessment class in seminary, but it was delivered to a congregation of only three—two professors and a student whose roles were to evaluate the performance. The results of that one were not good. They told me I needed some extensive work before I was suitable for the pulpit and prescribed a lengthy course of study that prompted me to apply to law school instead. That sermon was in 1983. Since then, public speaking had been confined to talking to judges and juries. For each of those previous sermons, my preparation time had probably been 20 hours—writing thoughts, researching authoritative support, preparing a working outline, and finally rehearsing the final performance in front of a mirror so that each bodily motion was appropriate with the message being conveyed at the moment.

Now I had ten or fifteen minutes to prepare before speaking to a chapel filled with 50 people. But retreating to my office wasn't an option either. The people were already filing in for the next service. Pappy's was the first hand at the door. "Happy Thanksgiving! I'm Pappy Hoyle and this is our new Executive Director, Blake Barrow," he said as he passed the handshake down the line much more gently than he passed Bibles.

The panic-stricken realization hit me that I was stuck standing next to Pappy shaking hands of visitors instead of seeking out solitude for the processing of thoughts. My preparation time had just been cut in half.

After five or six new visitors, I recognized a very familiar face —it was Jeff Ray, a fellow lawyer with whom I had worked up a few litigation cases. Jeff was about my age, but he had gone to law school right after his undergraduate work while I stayed on for a Master of

Arts and then seminary, so he had at least five years more experience in trial work than I had. Jeff had already built up his own law firm and his name was the first one on the door.

"Hey, I heard you had taken this job! Great for you! Congratulations!"

"Thank you."

"Show me around. I want to see what you are doing."

I looked at Pappy and then gave a reluctant "OK." Preparation time just got chopped again, but at least I could escape from Pappy, who probably was going to suck up all my remaining preparation time anyway.

We started at my new office just inside the front door of the Mission. It already looked like a lawyer lived there with diplomas and certificates on the wall and legal files covering 90% of the desk surface not already occupied by the computer monitor and keyboard. From my office we went down the hall past the counseling offices and into the women's and children's area, then back through the kitchen and dining hall to the men's dormitory at the other end of the building. It had to be one of the quickest tours I have ever given of our 14,000 square-foot building.

We returned to the open door at the rear of the chapel. Everyone was standing singing "Amazing Grace." Pappy was at the front by the pulpit leading the singing, and there was an empty chair beside him with my name on it facing toward the crowd. Jeff found one of the few vacant seats, and I walked down the center aisle to my designated spot.

Although everyone else was standing, I took a seat and opened Pappy's Bible that I was still carrying with me. I figured I had at least the time of one more verse of "Amazing Grace" and maybe two. "OK, Jesus, this better be good. Show me what to do."

I thought Luke would be a good place to start. How about the story of the two criminals on the crosses next to Jesus? Let's see, where is that? I flipped through a few pages near the end of Luke frantically searching for key words. One verse just ended, and, thanks be to God, Pappy just started on another one.

Pappy's baritone voice boomed out "When we've been there ten thousand years, bright shining as the sun..."

I love that verse even though it was not from the original writer, and, therefore, it was never included in the Methodist hymnals that I was raised on. But I also knew that Baptists *always* sang that verse last. I had less than thirty seconds to go.

Here it is! Chapter 23, beginning at verse 39. I read through the passage down to verse 43 where Jesus said, "Verily I say unto thee, today shalt thou be with me in Paradise." Pappy read, preached, and prayed in the King James.

Just as I finished reading, the music stopped and Pappy's voice announced, "Today we are blessed to hear from our new Executive Director, Blake Barrow."

I was on.

At least 50 people were waiting to hear the inspired words that their new leader had prepared. There was no microphone either, so I couldn't be timid. It was time to stand up straight, take a deep breath, push the air from the diaphragm and project the voice boldly and clearly so that the man who is hard of hearing on the back row can understand—Speech class 101.

"Good morning and God bless you all this beautiful Thanksgiving Day! I want to read you a short story about Jesus which has been a blessing to me. You will recall that when Jesus was crucified, there were three crosses. Jesus was in the middle with two others on each side sentenced to die with him."

Then I began reading at verse 39 from Pappy's Bible. I pointed out how even though we commonly refer to the two others as the thieves on the cross, Luke didn't tell us what they had done. He just referred to them as criminals or evil doers. Then, when one of them asked Jesus to remember him when Jesus came into his Kingdom, Jesus didn't first say, "Well let's talk about what awful things you have done to put yourself here. I am not so sure you are deserving of my Kingdom." Maybe Jesus already knew, but I think the past mistakes really were not that important to Jesus. At least they were not as important as the humble confession of "I deserve to be here."

I went on as to how there were no magic words that the man had to say. He didn't recite the sinner's prayer; it was just a very humble and sincere, "Jesus remember me." (Sort of like my prayer of "Jesus help—and this better be good.") There was certainly no action that the man needed to take to work off his sins. There was nothing that he could have done while nailed to the rough boards of his cross.

As I continued, it seemed as if I was just speaking out the next thought that popped into my head, and it actually seemed to flow in a meaningful fashion. With no notes to try to follow, there was nothing getting in the way of my making direct eye contact with the people and just talking directly to them about how Jesus wants to share his space in Paradise with us even though we may have committed deeds so terrible that we are deserving of the death penalty.

I recited a number of things that I had to be thankful for and concluded that as great as those blessings are, none of them are as wonderful as Jesus' message that he wants to share his space in Paradise with me.

"You may be living in a shelter. You may have nothing by the standards of this world, but Jesus wants to share Paradise with you, and, by comparison, nothing else is important."

Pappy had just provided the example of a Baptist altar call in the previous service, so I did my best to copy it. Then I turned to Pappy and asked if he would lead us in a closing hymn. He looked back at me and smiled for a couple of seconds with a look that told me I had passed; then he rose to direct the final song.

I never spoke with Pappy about why he did things the way he did that day. I really don't know if he was intentionally putting me on the spot, or if the test had been done completely on a subconscious level, although I have often reflected on the great gift he gave me. I was like the little kid approaching the cold swimming pool and thinking about dipping one toe into the water. Then Pappy came along and just picked me up and threw me directly into the deep end—swim or sink and adjust very quickly to the temperature of the water.

CHAPTER 3

THANK YOU

I LOVE THE STORY ABOUT Jesus' healing ten people and only one returned to say "thank you." I am not doing that well, but when I do receive a sincere thanks, it recharges me to keep going for several more years.

As my phone rang, I glanced at the caller ID and saw that the call was coming from somewhere in Florida. A female voice was on the other end. When she told me her name, I remembered who she was. I had not seen her for over ten years. She had been a Mission guest along with her mother and siblings.

My first introduction to the nonprofit world had come through Myrna Deckert several years before James Carroll introduced me to the Mission. She was the CEO of the El Paso YWCA. I was working for a lawyer who had filed a lawsuit against the Y. With a few hours notice, he handed me a file and instructed me to represent our client at a mediation. I read through all of the documents, met my client, and traveled to the mediator's office where I spent the next five hours sitting across the table from Myrna Deckert. I do not believe any Christian could sit at the same table with Myrna Deckert for five hours and not be transformed into a worker for the Kingdom of God.

I later researched her background. Over the course of 40 years, Myrna Deckert had built the El Paso YWCA from a relatively small nonprofit to the largest YWCA in the United States, and I had thought they were only a gym for women. I soon discovered that they were providing housing for homeless women, healthcare, daycare for children, and a huge range of other services to help the poor.

At the end of the day, the case reached a settlement. I had fulfilled my legal duty of representing my client to the best of my abilities; nevertheless, I had an overwhelming sense of shame listening to my client's excuses as to why she was too injured to return to work. At one point Myrna looked her straight in the eye and asked her if she really wanted a job. Her hesitant response said it all. When it was all done, Myrna had agreed to sign on the payment to my client so as to avoid going to court, but her comments of having to curtail several programs to help poor women and children pierced me to the heart. I vowed to myself to repay the entire settlement cost.

After all the documents were signed, I called Myrna and requested a tour of her latest project which was the women's transitional living center. Before she had a chance to turn me away, I offered to do free legal work for any woman who was living at the shelter. She consented to giving me the tour, but I sensed that she still felt like she was dancing with the devil.

I went back to my office and wrote her a letter of thanks for the tour and enclosed a contribution check for $5000. After another month went by and I had still not heard back from her, I called Myrna and told her that I knew she had women who needed legal assistance and that I was offering to do it all free of charge.

Two days later Myrna called me back, inviting me to meet Patricia, who had a court hearing the next day. Patricia had four children from two husbands. Both of the husbands had abandoned her, and child protective services now had custody of all four children. The next court hearing was at 9:00 a.m. the next morning and was to terminate her parental rights and put all the children up for adoption.

All of my legal career had been spent in personal injury trial work. Even though I had volunteered for the task, this job was quite a bit more than I was planning on. I had never done a termination of parental rights case and wasn't even sure of the legal standards. I stood in front of the judge and argued that a mother's right to raise her children is a fundamental right protected by the penumbra of the United States Constitution. Apparently the judge was so baffled by the line that he delayed all rulings for months, which was long enough for Patricia to demonstrate that she could provide a more stable environment for her children.

By the time the case was finished several years later, I had easily spent more than 1,000 hours in the legal fight for Patricia and her children. Patricia had all four of her children back with her. While all would agree that she had her issues and was never the perfect parent, she was their mother, and she loved her children dearly. No foster care setting could replace that mother's love.

As the case was still going, Patricia married a man who appeared to offer a stable setting for the kids. But I soon discovered that he had a problem with occasional drinking binges, and he turned violent when he was drunk.

One day Patricia and her children showed up at the Mission around 4:00 p.m. She told me her husband had gotten drunk and they needed to get away. The kids were two boys and two girls between the ages of 7 and 13, so they posed a housing challenge. To make matters worse, all of our beds were filled on the women's and children's side of the Mission.

I gathered some lifting help and moved my desk and office chairs into the foyer so Patricia and her kids could sleep on the floor of my office.

Over the next three years they returned to the Mission at least a half dozen times. Each stay was for four or five days. Then they would try going home again.

The voice on the phone was from one of her daughters. She was 20 years old and was living in Florida with her mom. She had looked me up on the internet and was calling to see if I was OK and to say "thank you."

Another five years have now passed since that call. I still remember the sound of her voice on the phone. Her call told me that she will never forget the love she was shown when she was a frightened eleven-year-old girl running from danger but not knowing where her mother was taking her. I will never forget that each time a young child comes into the Mission, that child is scared of what the future may hold and is in need of the calm assurance that the Mission is a safe place where the love of Jesus resides. The sound of her "thank you" resonates in my brain and fuels the encouragement that energizes me to reach out to one hundred more hurting children just like her.

CHAPTER 4

JACK WARD

JACK WARD WAS ONE OF the first new employees I hired at the Mission. He appeared at the door of my office asking for a job. He was tall and slender, and he carried a black leather Bible under his arm. We talked for a while about his talents and the jobs he had done. He was living in an economical apartment downtown, but if he was going to be able to keep it, he needed to earn some rent money. He was already familiar with the Rescue Mission as he had been one of our homeless guests several times in the past. In fact, since I was so new on the job, he really knew more about the Mission than I did. Apparently Pappy had been a great influence on him; his Bible looked just like Pappy's.

We did have an employment need at the time. I needed someone to sort through the donated clothing, separate things by sizes, and then distribute the clothes to people in need. The real challenge to the job was making sure that the people in need got what they needed, while the person who needed one coat didn't walk away with three. I had heard a story just a few weeks before about a man who took more clothing than he really needed. He sold the surplus for drug money and then died with an overdose. His widow was still living at the Mission.

Jack seemed up to the task, so I put him to work that afternoon. Some of his earlier jobs were in sales, and his organizational skills were pretty good. The first couple of weeks seemed to be going well both for Jack and the Mission.

One day I noticed that Jack seemed a little disoriented, but I was concentrating on other problems and didn't give the issue a lot of attention. The next day Jack was much worse. He had come to work but wandered around aimlessly as if he didn't know what he was supposed to be doing. Around noon one of our workers decided she needed to drive him to the hospital. By the time he arrived at the emergency room, he didn't even know his name, and he lapsed into a coma within two hours.

The medical news the next day was that Jack probably would not survive. He had told some of us that he had a daughter, so I began a frantic search to locate a relative. From the comments that he had made to some staff members, we assumed that the daughter would have been about 25 years old. Jack had left his Bible in his work area. I opened it up and scanned the inside covers for any information that would assist in finding his family. There was a lady's name and a phone number written on the flyleaf. I called the number to discover that she was a lady Jack met in church, and she really knew less about Jack than I did. He had a few notes tucked into the Bible but nothing that would lead me to a relative.

One of our counselors knew where his apartment was and gave me the address. The only other option I had was to look through the things in his apartment for clues. The apartment was only about three miles away. I drove to it and knocked on the door of the manager's office.

I was only about halfway through explaining the situation when the apartment manager stopped me. "I know who you are. I read about you in the paper. You are the lawyer who went to work at the Mission to help the poor. Come with me. I'll open the apartment for you."

Jack's apartment was only one room. He had a bed, a table, a closet, and a chair. He shared the bathroom with the person in the next room. If there was anything here that could help me, it wouldn't take too long to find it.

There were no skeletons in the closet. I found another Bible and a copy of *Pilgrim's Progress*. This Bible contained no notes at all, but tucked between its pages was a draft of a letter Jack had written to the nurses at Thomason Hospital, thanking them for caring for him when he had a stroke five years before. Evidently, Jack knew his body was a ticking time bomb. Yet there was still nothing to lead me to the identity of Jack's daughter, wife, former wife, or anyone else who may have been important to him.

Then I hit the most promising lead yet. Tucked away in his closet was a business card book. On the first page was Jack's own business card from a sales job he had held in Las Vegas. I proudly showed this goldmine of information to the apartment manager, advised him that he could lock the room back up, and quickly drove back to the Mission to start making phone calls.

I started with the number on Jack's own business card. The person answering the phone confirmed that Jack worked there in sales about two years before. I explained my desperation in trying to find a relative as we were running out of time. The doctors were now telling us that Jack had less than two days to live. The former employer agreed to pull Jack's personnel file and read to me what Jack wrote on the job application. Sure enough, they had a line for "person to contact in case of emergency." Jack had written in the name of a lady and her phone number. I excitedly took down the information hoping that person was his daughter, thanked him for his help, and then dialed the number that he had given me.

No answer.

So I started through the dozens of other business cards in his book. Most of the people on the other end of my phone calls confirmed that Jack used to sell business supplies, but, otherwise, they really knew nothing else about him. After about fifteen of those calls, I tried the "person to contact in case of emergency" again. This time a woman answered the phone. But she was not his daughter. She seemed surprised that she had been listed as the emergency contact. She said that she had lived in the apartment next door to Jack a few years before. She also had heard that he had a daughter, but she didn't even know the daughter's name or where she might be living.

Shortly after I hung up, Charles Bennet came into my office. He was living at the Mission and was working as our chaplain's assistant.

"You know, you are wasting a lot of time and money on long-distance phone calls trying to find one of Jack's relatives. If Jack had wanted you to find relatives, you would have found them by now. You see, Jack is just like me. We don't have any family other than the people here at this Mission. My real family didn't want me. I don't know why. That's just the way it is. And Jack is the same way."

I leaned back in my chair and closed the business card book. I had spent almost two days searching and made at least thirty phone calls. I had nothing to show for it. Charles was right.

Sometimes when the pressures of the law practice had gotten too great, I would pack up my camping gear and drive up into the mountains where I could take a hike through the woods or just sit under a tree and think without interruptions. I thought I was getting away to be alone.

Jack taught me that I had never really known what it was like to be alone. Being alone means having no one who really cares if you are alive or dead.

Jack Ward died the next day. We took up a collection at the Mission and held a funeral service in our chapel. It was attended by the only real family that Jack had—the people who were homeless at the Rescue Mission.

CHAPTER 5

BE MY FRIEND

I WAS GIVING A TOUR of the Mission to a group of four ladies. When we got to the women's and children's side of the Mission, we met a young lady named Jamie, and I introduced her to the ladies on my tour. Having such a small group for the tour allowed them the opportunity for questions directed to our guests that a larger group might not have had.

Onc of the ladies asked Jamie, "What do you need?"

She was probably expecting a response of, "Winter is coming, and I don't have a coat," or "It would be great to have eggs and sausage for breakfast." Solutions to such problems are very easy and require a minimal investment of time or money. Most of us have three times as many coats in our closets than we can wear.

Instead, her response shocked them all and demanded far more from them than the donation of a coat or food. She replied without any hesitation, "Be my friend."

Jamie was 21 years old and had been homeless since she was 9. She had numerous tattoos. A few weeks after she came to the Mission, she showed me her sketch book, which had magnificent artwork in it. At that time her vocational aspiration was to be a tattoo artist. Coming from her background, making tattoos was the only expression that she knew for her artistic abilities.

As she grew into adulthood, one of her tattoos really bothered her. She had a tattoo on the back of her right hand that looked like a set of brass knuckles.

Her husband had accepted Jesus as his savior at the Mission and started coming to church. She had come with him for a few weeks and then stopped coming.

When I asked her why she was no longer coming to church, she said that every time she shook hands with someone, their eyes immediately went to the tattoos on her hand, and she could see the expressions on their faces change. She said that she felt like everyone was judging her because of her past. Then she thanked me for accepting her from our first meeting, regardless of what she looked like.

CHAPTER 6

RESCUE ADS

I LEARNED VERY QUICKLY THAT marketing the Rescue Mission was very different from marketing another type of business in one respect: The purchaser of the product is not the consumer of the product. If I go the the grocery store and buy a carton of ice cream, I get an immediate feedback on the quality of my decision as I eat the ice cream. However, in the case of the Mission, the purchaser is the donor who wants to help people who are homeless, and the consumer is the person who is homeless. They are not the same. The marketing challenge is to keep the purchasers informed as to the quality of services they have purchased even though they have not experienced those services themselves.

One of our efforts to get the word out about the work of the Rescue Mission was to write a small newspaper called the *Rescue Reporter*. I had different staff members write articles about their work in their section of the Mission. One of our counselors wrote about our drug and alcohol rehabilitation program. Our chaplain wrote about how one of our Mission guests developed a whole new value system after accepting Jesus as his savior. I wrote the cover article on how people in our community can provide meaningful help for those who are homeless.

The entire spread was eight pages. We included pictures of people at the Mission and a few advertisements from businesses that supported the Mission. The idea was to introduce the Mission to people who were not already on our mailing list, so that more people in El Paso could understand and support the work of the Mission. Each copy had an envelope included for people to mail in a contribution if they liked what they read.

The next challenge was how to distribute the newspaper. We were able to get enough advertisement revenue to cover the costs of paper and printing. The post office had provided a list of how many households were in each zip code in El Paso. We added up the costs of letting the post office deliver a copy to every home but concluded that it was too high. Then I had a brainstorm—we could deliver the paper ourselves using labor from our own guests by putting the papers into plastic bags and hanging them on doorknobs. I pulled out my calculator and started crunching numbers. If a person could walk down a residential street and hang three bags on front doors in a minute, then that person would be hanging 180 in an hour and a little over 1000 in a six-hour day. Of course, apartment complexes could be covered much faster, and areas with large residential lots would be slower. But very few areas of El Paso have big yards due to the expense of watering grass in the desert.

If we paid our workers at minimum wage for a seven-hour shift, bought them lunch on the road, and had them delivering for six hours, our costs of delivery per paper would be between four and five cents. We also had to add in fuel costs and the time of the van driver. Our van was big enough to take eight to ten people out at a time along with their backpacks filled with papers. We would still be substantially below postage rates.

I found out where to order plastic bags with a hole in the top for hanging on doorknobs. Two hundred thousand papers would cover about 75% of the households in El Paso. If we could average 8000 papers delivered each day, we could distribute all 200,000 papers in 25 days. I ordered the papers and plastic bags. If we could start delivering papers around October 25, all papers could be delivered by Thanksgiving, even if we took weekends off.

The first task once the papers and plastic bags arrived was to insert the donation envelope into each paper and then place each paper into a plastic bag. By this time word had spread around the Mission about the newspaper bagging and delivery jobs that were coming. I had people signing up to work even before the first truckload of papers arrived.

I gave priority for the envelope and paper-stuffing jobs to those who were too disabled to walk through the neighborhoods. I structured the stuffing jobs at a fixed price for the preparation of 1000 papers. In that manner the very disabled people could work at a slower pace, and we still paid the same price per piece.

We had a large map of El Paso posted on the wall, and the van driver had his own map. Once a street was covered, the driver would mark it with his highlighter. When he returned at the end of the day, I would take his map and mark off the covered streets on the big wall map. Then we would plan out which streets to attack the next day.

We quickly worked up an efficient delivery system. Most neighborhoods had parallel streets. Our workers were divided into pairs. We dropped off a pair of workers at the top of each street so that most of the walking was down hill. Each worker would take one side of the street, and they would meet at the bottom. The van was in continual motion. Once the driver dropped off the fourth or fifth pair of workers, he would circle to the bottom of the streets and start picking up the earlier pairs to carry them to the next streets.

Before long, workers started keeping track of how many papers they had distributed and competing with each other to see which one of the pair could hit every house and get to the bottom of the street first. More than a few friendly wagers were made as to who could pass out the most papers. One of our men boasted that he was the best of the crew at over 1300 papers for each day that he worked.

I usually organized the groups in the mornings, signed in all of the workers for payroll calculations, and made sure that all of the needed supplies were loaded in the van. Anytime you gather a group of people to perform a task over any significant length of time, someone will rise to a leadership position and become the informal crew chief. Mark was just such a "take charge" kind of person. He was sitting in the front passenger seat so that he could share strategy ideas with the driver. As I was standing at the open side door of the van writing down the names of all our workers, Mark turned around and exclaimed: "Oh no, we will be moving slower today. We have a girl on the crew."

At the end of the day that group of ten workers had hit 14,350 houses. They ran out of papers by one o'clock and had to return to the Mission to load up several thousand more. It was a record that stood until all 200,000 had been distributed. It was a good thing they all had tennis shoes on. The "girl" was a 35 year-old woman who was suddenly motivated to whip every man on the van. They were all running from house to house for the entire shift.

I was embarrassed that morning at Mark's politically incorrect comment. But, at the end of the day, I realized that this homeless man was a personnel management genius. He knew exactly what he was doing. He was setting up the competition and made careful note of which men could not keep up with the "girl."

We kept a daily count of how many papers had been distributed to stay on schedule to have all of the papers delivered before Thanksgiving. We did work two Saturdays to catch up, and the last paper was delivered on the Wednesday before Thanksgiving.

Thanksgiving was always a huge celebration at the Rescue Mission. The people who have the least always seem to be the most appreciative for the limited blessings that they do have. I came into the Mission that Thanksgiving morning feeling very thankful myself. The kitchen staff had prepared a great feast, and I was thrilled and relieved that we had completed this huge task of hand-delivering 200,000 papers.

To my surprise, however, very few residents of the Mission shared my excitement. In fact, I had never seen so many dejected looking people. I quickly realized that while I was elated at the accomplishment of mobilizing a homeless workforce and completing this task on time, they understood the arrival of Thanksgiving to mean that they were out of a job.

It was an experience of looking at the same event through someone else's eyes. To me, the task of stuffing envelopes into papers, papers into plastic bags, and then hanging them one at a time on doorknobs was boring and a lot of walking. For our homeless workforce, on the other hand, it was an opportunity to earn a paycheck when no other jobs were available, and the task was meaningful since it supported the Mission which was providing them with food and shelter. To the extent that the job lacked mental stimulation, they made up competitive games to challenge each other.

Unfortunately, the people in our society who make employment decisions tend to look at things the way I had done. They try to minimize the tasks that they personally find boring, while the people actually doing those tasks may find meaning in them and take great pride in the work they are doing.

We followed our Thanksgiving routine of bringing people into the chapel and then dismissing them to the dining room. By the time the second Thanksgiving service started, I had spoken to enough people to know what I had to do. I stood up in the next Thanksgiving service and announced that I was thankful for the start of our new business, called Rescue Ads. We would get local businesses to purchase advertising fliers, which would be stuffed into plastic bags just like we had done for our newspaper. Then we would walk through neighborhoods and hang the bags on people's doors.

"If you are able to walk down a street with a backpack of plastic bags and hang one on each door, you can have a job!"

The spirit of Thanksgiving returned.

CHAPTER 7

$2.95 CRAYOLAS

EACH YEAR, JUST BEFORE THE start of school, I call all of the kids up to the front of the Mission for a school clothing and supplies discussion. Most of our kids are really excited about returning to school—even if it means that they are moving to a new school and have to start the process all over again of meeting new people and making new friends.

Every child has to have something new to go to school with —something that he or she can feel good about. I have a theory that kids learn better if they feel good about themselves. Perhaps my "theory" borders so much on the obvious that I have never felt the need to create a control group of kids who got nothing but someone else's cast-offs that landed in the Mission's donation bin, while other kids got all new stuff.

Shoes are usually the greatest in demand. The kids' feet grow so fast that the shoes that fit six months ago are now one full size too small—and those shoes were usually well-worn when they were acquired. A few of our kids have never been to a shoe store for a new pair of shoes. If a child does have a good pair of shoes, then maybe some new blue jeans are in order. If we don't have too many kids, or if there is a little surplus in the monthly budget, I will do both.

My favorite shopping spot is Big 5. The store is not so large that I am in danger of losing children if I take five or six at one time, and they have a great selection of children's shoes. I know the manager by first name, and when he sees me coming, he knows where all the kids are from. Besides, I come in with a new set of kids each August and not too many of them look like me. As soon as we walk in the door and head toward the shoes on the rear wall of the store, Craig will appear and give us personal service. Of course, none of the kids know their real shoe size, so every foot has to be measured. Usually I have to buy a big bag of socks, since the socks on their feet simply are not going to go in and out of new shoes. Craig always seems very pleased when I say, "I think we will need some new socks too. Would you mind if we just open up the packages and give everyone new socks first?"

The best part of going to Big 5 is that I never have walked into the store when children's shoes are not on sale—and what a huge sale it is! Funny thing, I never see the big sale advertised in the newspaper, and the sale prices are not on the shoe boxes either. Craig will bring out a new pair of shoes and hand me the box. I will turn the box on its end looking for the price which might be $29.95. Craig will say, "No, these are on sale today for $9.95." Then he retreats to the back of the store for more shoe boxes while I fit kids with shoes. Regardless of which shoes a child likes, they are always on sale.

At the end of the shopping trip, each child goes back into the Mission van carrying a shopping bag. Of course, all of the kids wear their new shoes. When they find a pair that they like and I give my nod of approval that the shoes are the right size, they will not take them off again, so the shopping bags contain only the old shoes. As soon as the van pulls up to the Mission and I open the door, the kids will run off to find their mothers and show off their new shoes. Occasionally we have a child at the Mission with a single father, but most of the kids are with their mothers. Very rarely do we get husbands and wives together with kids. Stable, two-parent families are a powerful weapon against homelessness.

Once school has started and the kids receive their teachers' supplies list, we have to go back to the store. This trip is usually to Target where we will find notebooks, pencils, pens, backpacks, etc. Target is also a great source for kids' blue jeans. But, unlike Big 5, there never is a surprise sale.

Cindy had come to the Mission a little late for the first day of school, so when we went to Target for supplies, it was just the two of us. She had her pre-printed, official supplies list from her teacher—everything a first-grader will need. Spiral notebooks with the lines spaced just so far apart, pencils, the big erasers that actually worked instead of relying on the little ones at the ends of the pencils. The list went on. As we were filling our cart with the not-so-exciting essentials, I noticed Cindy looking at the Crayola rack. Crayolas were not on the list of essentials, and we had a bucket full of used crayons at the Mission. Most of them were broken and the paper wrappers were gone, but they did the job for an artistic child who had nothing else.

Cindy looked up at me and then very tentatively reached her hand out to pick up a box of brand new Crayola crayons with eight different colors in the box. Target had the display arranged with the larger boxes on the left and the smaller ones on the right—all at a first-grader's eye level. Cindy had picked up the smallest box of eight and just looked up at me without saying a word.

I quickly glanced across the Crayola display noticing the price differences between the boxes of 8, 24, and 48 crayons.

"No, Cindy," I said as I took the box from her hand and put it back on the shelf.

"I think you need this one." I handed her the 48-count box. I didn't remember their being that cheap when I was a kid. It was only $2.95. Nor do I remember ever getting a new 48-color box myself, but the price of such luxury obviously had declined over the years.

Cindy's eyes got really wide, and she just stared at me for a few seconds as if she had been hit in the face with cold water. Then she lunged at me, grabbing my right leg just above the knee and squeezing as hard as she could. I thought she was cutting off the circulation in my leg, and then I realized that both of her feet were standing on my right foot.

I tried to wipe my eyes, but I didn't have a Kleenex in my pocket. I looked around to see if any customers were watching a grown man wiping away his tears with a little kid standing on his foot. It was such a little thing. What else could you buy for $2.95? How could I have imagined that it would mean so much to little Cindy?

After about twenty seconds I gained the composure to say, "Uh, Cindy, the notebooks are on this next aisle."

She was still attached to my leg like a python. I tried to start walking, but she still wouldn't let go, so I limped to the next aisle —stiffening my ankle with each step to lift Cindy up and putting in the extra effort of lifting a 40-pound, one-sided appendage. Take a step with the left foot. Lift Cindy with the right. Take a step with the left foot. Lift Cindy with the right. Finally, she let go after about ten minutes, and we could proceed to the checkout.

I am frequently asked, "What can I do to make a meaningful difference for a person who is homeless? I don't have much time, and I don't have much money."

Do you have an hour? Do you have $2.95? Would you like to send a message that says "I care" and "You are important" to a homeless child who has nothing. Have you bought a box of crayons recently?

CHAPTER 8

PGA LESSON

JIM WAS SEATED OUTSIDE MY office reading one of my old *Golf Digest* magazines that I had left on a table. I have not met many homeless men who had an interest in golf, so I asked if he played. Jim told me he had been working as a caddie on the PGA tour. I have heard many stories of where our homeless guests have been, but I was a bit skeptical of this one.

He appeared to be in his mid-thirties and didn't look particularly athletic. His story gained some credibility when he started naming some of the touring pros that he had caddied for and telling me about their particular idiosyncrasies.

He told me that he had been carrying a pro's bag down a steep hill when he turned abruptly and felt something snap in his knee. He was able to limp through the remaining holes but was not able to walk the next day. A few months later, he had surgery to repair a torn ligament.

While the job may seem glamorous, a PGA tour caddie is not far from homelessness, even without a busted knee. Why have a home? All of his things would fit in his car, and he lived in motels near the various golf courses. Monday and Tuesday were traveling days to get to the next tournament. Wednesday was the practice round, and the competition started all over again on Thursday morning. If there was not an affordable motel near the course, he would sleep in his car.

A caddie's tip is typically 10% of the pro's winnings, but if the guy you are carrying for doesn't make the cut, you may be begging for gas money to get to the next stop.

The MRI center wanted its payment up front. He found a sympathetic surgeon who would take payments after $500 down, but he had to pay the hospital in full before the operation.

He thought he had been frugal in saving up some funds whenever his team finished in the money, but medical expenses and a motel room to rest his leg quickly wiped it out. He had met a friend in California where he thought he could stay for a while, so he budgeted his last dollars for enough gas to drive to California. That plan went terribly wrong when the transmission in his car died as he was rolling through El Paso. It was far from new when he bought it, and 30,000 miles a year had finally done it in. He came to the Rescue Mission with only what he could carry in his hands.

My own golf time had suffered a terrible hit a year before. I had been supervising the off-loading of a piece of equipment from our flatbed trailer. I was standing on the trailer directing the forklift driver exactly where to place the forks so as not to damage this 1500-pound machine. As he raised the forks, the machine started slipping, so I jumped in front of it to try to shove it back onto the forklift. After a half of a second, I realized I was in a losing battle and pushed away from it with my right arm. The machine slid off of the forks and crashed to the bed of the trailer as my right hand was still pushing against it. My hand was not caught on it, but the momentum of the machine falling from the forklift was more than my body could take. I could feel my arm bone being ripped out of the shoulder socket.

For several weeks I could not lift my right arm to the level of my face. I learned to eat, shave, and brush my teeth with my left hand.

Our District Conference for the Association of Gospel Rescue Missions that year was held in Longview, Texas. After a few hours of meetings, we adjourned to the adjacent 9-hole golf course. It was a beautiful track which followed both sides of a tree-lined creek bed. I started out walking the course with my friends but couldn't stand the pain of just watching and not being able to play. When we got to the fourth tee, I asked if I could borrow a ball and a three-wood. After a little range-of-motion experimentation, I found that I could use the right hand to help guide the club in the first half of the backswing, but then I had to release the right hand, take the club back, and swing through with the left alone. The first shot was a pathetic fade, but then I got the hang of it. I actually won a hole swinging with one arm, although after three holes, my shoulder was in such intense pain that I had to quit.

From my experience as a personal injury lawyer, I knew most of the orthopedic surgeons in the area. Dr. Dickason was my shoulder expert of choice, and he did a magnificent job reconstructing my shoulder. Of course, it really helps to have over 100 homeless people praying for your rapid recovery. Within three days of the surgery, I had close to full range-of-motion in my shoulder. In spite of my practically miraculous shoulder flexibility, Dr. Dickason warned me to take it slowly. About a month had passed since the surgery, and I had not yet tried a full golf swing again.

We traded golf stories for a while and shared about our favorite places to play. He enjoyed Pebble Beach and Torrey Pines, but he wasn't sure if he would be able to hike the elevation changes again.

Then the thought hit me as I was talking with Jim: "You

don't know if you can still hike 18. I don't know if I can swing. It's one o'clock in the afternoon. I play at a course built on the side of Franklin Mountain. If you can walk that 18, you are ready to return to the tour. Let's go."

I could carry my own golf bag without putting any pressure on the surgery site, so I told him not to worry about the bag. Jim just needed to think about his knee while walking up, down, and side hills.

Jim was quiet for the first three holes. When I skulled a chip shot across the fourth green, Jim couldn't hold his tongue any longer.

"Looks like you tried to scoop that one."

"What do you mean?"

"The natural tendency is to try to help the ball up on a short chip. But that is the worst thing you can do. You will either hit the ground in front of the ball or blade it. Play it farther back in your stance so that the club head is moving down as it strikes the ball."

I tossed another ball on the ground and tried it again from farther back in the stance. The ball popped up and rolled about ten feet past the cup.

"Great! Now, put the thought in your mind that you need to turn your shoulders on the chip and swing with your body turn. Just let your arms and hands follow the shoulder turn."

I dropped another ball on the ground and tried again. This one rolled to within four feet of the cup. I was impressed.

After I thanked him for the first few tips, Jim opened up with more pointers to help me out. When we had arrived at the course, I still wasn't sure if Jim was for real. After all, how many guys who are on TV each weekend wind up in homeless shelters? He proceeded to give me a dozen or more tips, and each one of them was just what I needed to hear.

Even if I made a bad shot, Jim had something encouraging to say.

"That was a pretty big fade, but you made solid contact. As long as you are making solid contact, steering the ball is easy. Put this thought in your head: instead of starting the club straight back, turn it to the inside at the start of the backswing. Then your swing will be more inside-out, and your shot will turn a little to the left. On the follow-through, the club will follow the same path as the backswing."

I dropped another ball and hit it thinking about taking an inside path on the backswing. This one went straight at the pin.

After a few more shots, he had more advice: "That was a great swing, but you lifted your head a little as you swung through. Remember, if you pick your head up to see where your ball is going, you are not going to like what you see. Keep your head down, and I will watch the ball for you."

As the lessons and the encouragement kept coming, I began to get the feeling that I could win any tournament as long as I had Jim at my side. Not only had this guy been telling me the truth about his life, but he was very good at his job.

I could swing a club again. Jim could walk 18, and both of us were feeling really good.

When we left the 18th green, I pulled out my wallet and gave Jim a tip with all the bills I had left in it, which wasn't much compared to the value of the experience. It was one of the best golf lessons I ever had.

I found a note taped to my door the next morning. Jim had written to thank me for the afternoon. Then, to my great disappointment, he wrote that now that he knew he could walk 18, he was hitchhiking to Florida to catch the next tour stop.

Jim, if you are reading this book. I am sorry that I didn't have any more money with me. If you come back for another lesson, I will do better.

CHAPTER 9

I'M THE BEST DAD HE'S GOT

ONE OF MY FAVORITE ACTIVITIES is taking all of the children we have at the Mission to the Amigo Air Show each October. I discovered a trick so that I would not lose any children. I would buy bright colored baseball caps that were all the same color. I had to get a color that no one else had. Neon green worked well. Each child had to wear a cap. I could look out over the crowds of thousands of people at the air show and count the caps. I have taken a dozen kids to the air show all by myself, and I have never lost a child.

I remember the day that Santana and Vicki, his mother, came to the Mission. It was the Monday after the air show, and I was sorry he had missed it. We already had a crowd of ten children between the ages of four and eleven that I had taken to the show. The children's side of the Mission was pretty full, but there would have been room for one more kid in the van.

Our counselors told me their story after they had checked in. Santana was born in Midland, Texas, and was named for his father. Unfortunately, his father was apprehended by the Border Patrol and deported to Mexico. Vicki never heard from him again, and she and Santana soon became homeless. From the medical records that we later discovered, I know that they had been in the El Paso area for at least a year before coming to the Mission. Their previous three months had been spent at the Salvation Army. I don't know where they had been staying before that time.

As with most of the adults coming into the Mission, our counselors were pushing Vicki to get a job. The rehabilitation task is always more difficult for women with children than with single people because we need to place the mother in a job that generates enough income to provide for childcare in addition to all of their other living expenses. Fortunately, Santana was just barely old enough to enroll in pre-Kindergarten. I was able to get a copy of his shot record and then took him to the La Fe Clinic for additional shots so that we could place him in school.

Even though pre-K did not provide a full day's schedule, it occupied several hours that we would otherwise have had to fill with childcare. The goal was to provide proper care for Santana for at least nine hours a day, freeing Vicki to get a full-time job. It is always a challenge, particularly when there is very little money to start childcare so that the mother can start looking for the job. I became very good friends with the staff of El Paso Children's Daycare. Frequently, I would pay up for the first few weeks of childcare as an investment hoping that the mother would have a job before the time of my tuition payment had been used up.

Vicki posed an additional challenge. While we were doing everything we could to look after Santana during the working day, Vicki was doing nothing as far as looking for a job. El Paso Children's Daycare had positions available only for kids staying the full day, so all of us at the Mission were spending lots of time with Santana in the afternoons. When we pressed the employment issue with Vicki, she told us she had cancer.

I was doubtful about the diagnosis because she looked too good. She was very tall for an Hispanic woman at almost six feet and looked very healthy. Her weight was proportionate to her height. She simply did not look like any of the other cancer patients we had cared for.

My office was next to the front door of the Mission, and I usually worked with my door open as I preferred the feeling of open spaces. Santana would come into my office and spend lots of time in the chair in front of my desk. He had a brilliantly inquisitive mind and was constantly asking me questions. Most of them began with the word "why." One time he asked a question beginning with "how."

"How does the stuff you put into the keyboard go from the keyboard to the computer to the screen?"

He seemed greatly disappointed when he finally hit on a question that I had to say, "I really don't know."

When I got up from my chair to go tackle another task, Santana would climb up into my desk chair, stretch his arms out on the chair arms and try his best to fill my seat.

Santana came into my office one day and climbed into the chair in front of my desk. As usual he was talking nonstop and was filled with questions about why these things happened and how those things worked.

Then he blurted out, "Is it OK if I call you 'Dad?'"

I thought for a couple of seconds about that one and replied, "Uh, yea, that's OK."

But that response wasn't good enough for him.

"And will you call me 'Son?'"

"Uh, sure."

From that day forward, he never called me anything but "Dad."

One day when I arrived at work, one of our counselors told me that Vicki had started bleeding during the night and had gone to the hospital. Our Mission driver had already taken Santana to school, but I would need to go pick him up and keep him with me after pre-K.

After three days when Vicki had not yet returned from the hospital, I went to visit her to get an idea when she would be coming back to the Mission. The news was pretty dire. Indeed, she had cervical cancer. The tumor had grown to the point of blocking the ureters that led from the kidneys to the bladder. The doctor gave her the option of doing nothing, which meant that she would die within a few days, or she could have surgery to implant artificial ureters to go around the tumor. The surgery might extend her life for another six months, but her death would be slow and painful. Vicki had chosen the longer option.

I was in shock on hearing the news.

All that I could think of to ask was, "Who do you want us to call?"

"No one."

When I returned to the Mission and explained the situation to our staff, one of them had an idea of whom to call. El Paso has a medical clinic for persons who are homeless. These were the days before HIPAA, so after a couple of phone calls to find the right person, we were able to get a copy of all of her medical records from that clinic. Included in those records was a copy of a document from Thomason Hospital from eighteen months before. Indeed, at that time she had been diagnosed with cervical cancer. It had been discovered at an early stage when the probability of her surviving would have been very good if she had just received treatment. Now it was too late.

Included in the intake information sheet from the clinic records was that all-important line: "Person to contact in case of emergency."

Surprisingly, Vicki had listed her mother and father who were living about 400 miles south of El Paso in Mexico. Within a day we were able to contact them by phone. They were shocked to learn that their daughter was still alive, and then we had to tell them that she would not be alive much longer. No one in her family had heard from her in over five years. None of them knew that she had a son.

Vicki was discharged from the hospital the next day. We brought her back to the Mission and moved her into her own room which we had reserved for hospice patients. Even though she had been quite active before going to the hospital, I never saw her get out of bed again after she had received her death sentence.

Within another three days her family arrived. What a family it was! I discovered that Vicki was one of eight children, and half of them were living in the United States. Both parents and half of her siblings came into my office, and I got to speak with them first before taking them to Vicki's room. From the things they told me and the things that I had already learned from Vicki, I could piece together the puzzle. Vicki was so ashamed of the way that she had lived her life that she had chosen to crawl into a hole and die rather than to face the family that she felt she had disappointed.

The reunion was beautiful. None of her family members questioned her or criticized her about why she had run away and not contacted any of them in so long. They just reached out and loved her and welcomed her back. Vicki never asked me how we were able to find her family, or why we had contacted them after she told me not to call anyone, but I could see in her face that she was thrilled to see her mother and father again.

After a few days, Vicki's brothers and sisters returned to their homes, and Santana and I started spending even more time together. I think he preferred to be with me rather than with this new crowd of relatives that he had never met before.

On the first Saturday in December my wife and I and our two

kids were going shopping for a Christmas tree. I had been working at the Mission that morning and told my wife that I would be home before noon so that we could survey the Christmas tree lots. Our own two girls were 7 and 11 so the VW Vanagon was big enough for all of us and the new tree. We had no one to watch Santana that afternoon, so I brought him with me when I stopped at home to pick up my wife and kids.

My wife sat in the passenger's seat on my right and all of the kids were in the back. As usual, Santana kept talking nonstop while we were driving. Again, most of his sentences began with "why." We bought one tree for ourselves and another one to set up at the Mission. Then we went to get lunch. We pulled into a Whataburger, and I sent the kids off to the restroom to wash up. All of them had insisted on feeling the branches of every potential tree selection, and their hands were covered with sap. Once my wife and I were alone, she glared at me and demanded, "You mind telling me why this kid calls you Dad?"

"I don't mind," I replied, "I'm the best Dad he's got."

I had never noticed it before, but Santana did have a striking resemblance to me.

Once we all got to know Santana's great big, natural family, we discovered that he had an aunt and uncle in San Jose, California, who were not able to have children of their own. It was a great placement even though I was very sorry to see him go.

Vicki surprised us all by living another ten months instead of the six that the doctors had predicted. Either her mother or her father was at the side of her bed every minute of those ten months. They had left their home and moved into the Rescue Mission to hold her hand for all of the time that she had left.

Santana in Blake's Office

CHAPTER 10

I HAVE A JOB

LATE AFTERNOON ON A COLD winter day I walked by the front desk where an obviously intoxicated man was trying to check in. I had already learned the hard way that a shelter cannot serve the dual purposes of dry-out tank and rehabilitation center. You can spend months helping someone come clean and then destroy all that work in one moment by allowing another person to move in who smells like a brewery. The mere smell of the alcohol is enough to revive the uncontrollable temptations and send a person making progress over the edge.

It was getting cold and dark, and I felt sorry for this man whom I was about to turn away for the good of others under our roof. I interrupted his conversation with our receptionist.

"I am sorry, sir, but we can't let you stay in the Mission when you have been drinking since we are running a rehabilitation program here. But it is getting cold outside. I will be happy to give you a ride over to the Opportunity Center if you like. You are welcome to come back when you sober up."

The Opportunity Center is a shelter on the other side of downtown. They proclaimed their purpose was to offer shelter to persons who were homeless, whether or not those people were able or willing to address the issues that caused them to become homeless.

The man accepted my invitation, and we walked outside to my van. As we were driving away from the Mission, he said, "I don't know why you people at the Mission won't let me drink. You see, I am an alcoholic, and alcoholics have to drink."

He spoke in a manner indicating that he was perfectly accepting of his lot in life.

Then he continued in his slurred speech, "And I don't know why you people are always after me to go get a job. I have a job!"

Now he had my curiosity up. He had long, stringy hair that reached to the middle of his back and wore a blue jean jacket with stains and holes in it. I doubt he had taken a bath in a week. Who would have hired a man looking like this?

"Really," I said, "what is your job?"

He reached into his jacket and pulled out a piece of cardboard. When I saw the writing on the cardboard, my brain cells kicked in, and I remembered that I had seen him standing on a street corner. He had written on the cardboard:

WHY LIE?

I NEED A BEER

"I fly a sign!" he proclaimed with an air of pride at his vocational accomplishment.

"Amazing," I thought, "he views standing on a street corner

holding a piece of cardboard as his regular employment, and some people pay him to do it!"

He doesn't have to answer to a boss. He can show up for work whenever he likes, and as soon as he has collected enough money, he can take a break and go get another beer.

CHAPTER 11

DEMONS

I HAVE LONG SUFFERED FROM the delusion that if I can place myself inside a person's head so that I understand why that person is making the decisions he is making, then I will know how to press the right buttons to alter that decision-making process and help him make productive decisions instead of destructive ones. After sixteen years, my strategy has never worked, but I still keep trying.

I have recognized that sanity is a relative thing. In fact, many of my friends were convinced that I had lost mine by giving up a good-paying job to work in a homeless shelter. If sanity means thinking like most other people in this world and working to amass the greatest amount of wealth and gather the greatest number of toys, then I am pleased to be a dropout.

At least ninety-five percent of our guests are perfectly sane by my standards, but we do get a few who are way over the edge. Of all the really crazy people I have encountered, one woman stands out. She would speak with me, but none of her conversations made much sense. In fact, sometimes I got the impression that she was talking past me and speaking to someone else who wasn't there. Of course, I have met quite a few people who spoke nonsense, but this lady was different. Usually her conversation concerned something or someone who needed to die. Her eyes revealed more than her speech. Looking into her eyes was like peering into the depths of evil.

Fortunately, we had a professional counselor on our Board. I thought back to my first meeting with the Board on the day I was hired. All of the Board members introduced themselves very briefly. Basically the introduction was just name and occupation and maybe a few words about their involvement with the Board of the Mission. When we got to Walter Deines, I learned that he was a counselor. While I am generally terrible at remembering names, I parked that one in the back of my brain thinking that the day will come quickly when I will need to consult with him.

No time like the present. I grabbed my phone book, looked up the number and called Walter. The phone rang until it got to the "leave a message" line. So I left a message of perplexed frustration and waited for the call back.

The next day I was sitting in my office near the front door of the Mission when I recognized the voice of my chaplain screaming, "Come out of her in the name of Jesus!" He repeated it over and over until the woman retreated back to the women's dorm. I didn't even have to look out the door to see whom he was yelling at. It had to be the same woman I had met. I came out of my office in time to find him standing in the middle of the Mission foyer by himself with the woman having run away. Pappy had retired and we had a new chaplain. I suggested to him that he might try commanding the demon by pleading the blood of Jesus as opposed to the name of Jesus.

Of course Jesus cautioned us about casting out demons indiscriminately. If the person doesn't really want to be clean, the expelled demons will invite more demons into the cleansed house, and the end result will be worse than before. The time to clean house is when the person is willing to invite the Holy Spirit in. So I left the issue alone, but I watched her carefully.

Only a couple of days later we were holding a service in the chapel. I tried to gather as many people as I could for our chaplain. He and his entire family were very musical. He played the keyboard, one of his kids was on guitar, and another one was a great drummer. He would give short messages between the songs, but most of his preaching was actually done through the music. We had about thirty in attendance, including at least eight children. As I was standing at the back, listening to their music, this woman entered from the back and started gathering children like a mother hen to escort them out of the chapel.

She came up the center isle, grabbed a five year-old boy by the hand and whispered something in his ear. He got up and they walked to the back of the chapel. Then she left him to wait at the back door and returned to the front. About twenty seconds later she was walking to the back of the chapel with two more children—one on each hand. But when she got to the rear door, she discovered that the first child had returned to his old seat and was listening to the chaplain's music. I saw the look of frustration on her face as she left the two at the back door and went back for the first one. I watched her scowl at the first child and say something to him. He got up from his chair, and they both started to the back. This time, instead of holding his hand she was pushing him along with the palms of her hands, shoving him in the back. After she had moved about three rows of chairs toward the rear of the chapel, she reached out for a little girl who was sitting near the aisle. She grabbed her by the hand and was leading her to the back while still shoving the boy with her other hand.

Her expression of frustration turned to panic as she looked toward the rear door to discover that the two kids she had left there had also returned to their seats. She motioned for the two next to her to go to the back door as she turned to retrieve the other two.

By this time I had moved to the back door of the chapel to put an end to child removal. Our chaplain's music and the messages he gave between songs were so interesting that all of the kids wanted to hear it, but this woman had my full attention, and I was no longer listening to the music. Every now and then I glanced up from her to the chaplain's face. He was in the middle of a long song, and he didn't miss a beat, but he also could see what was happening with this woman herding children.

She was coming down the aisle to the back of the chapel again. This time she had three kids—one in each hand and another being herded in front of them. Her head was down watching the children, so she didn't see me until she was almost to the rear door. I was standing there holding the hands of the last two children. She looked up at me and was startled to see me there.

"The children are staying in the chapel." I looked at the oldest child, "You guys go sit down."

She dropped the hands of the two kids she was holding, and all of the children responded with an amazing obedience. Her countenance of frustration turned to anger as she looked at me and said, "No, no, the children need to leave; the children need to leave!"

"They are not leaving. They want to hear about Jesus."

When I said "Jesus," she bared her teeth and hissed at me like a snake, then fled from the chapel leaving all children safely behind.

Shortly after the service, my chaplain came to me. "What was that all about with that crazy woman, and how did you get her to go away?"

"Well, I think we have some real problems. She was gathering up all of the kids to get them out of the chapel."

But, now that the service was over, I was not so sure that our kids were any safer. They had gone back to the women's and children's dorm where the crazy lady was. Plus, I could not watch the kids while they were in the dorm and I was in my office. The kids had been safer in the chapel. Before she was just an annoyance. Now I felt like our kids may be in danger, and some stronger action was needed right away.

Well, I could call the police and tell them to escort her off of the property. I can see the police report now: "Woman expelled from the Rescue Mission because she likes to watch over children, and she hissed at the Director." No, that won't work.

I leaned back in my desk chair, stroking my chin, and praying for an answer. My chaplain was sitting silently in the chair in front of my desk. He was out of ideas as his exorcism attempt hadn't worked.

"I think I have an idea. Watch this," I said. "One of two things is about to happen, but I don't know which one."

Fortunately, we had just invested in an intercom system for the Mission. Now we could press a button and talk into a microphone and be heard over the entire building. The front desk clerk would use it to announce meal times, chapel services, or that someone had received a phone call. We had taken the extra step of wiring it to a CD player. My idea was that we could play soothing music over the intercom to inspire or at least settle the nerves of our guests. I thought it would be great to play Christmas carols in December and have everyone singing along. Little things like that go a long way when you have 120 anxious and frequently dejected people crammed into a small space.

I had just purchased a complete set of the New Testament on CDs. I opened up my folder of CDs and thought about where to start. "I think the Gospel of John will do just fine." I pulled out the CD starting with John and marched toward the front desk.

"Put this CD on the intercom and crank up the volume, please." I handed it to the front desk clerk.

After a few seconds a booming bass voice started speaking, resonating down the halls, through the kitchen, the dining room and the dormitories:

"IN THE BEGINNING WAS THE WORD AND THE WORD WAS WITH GOD AND THE WORD WAS GOD...."

I just stood by the front desk waiting in anticipation as to what would happen. It did not take long. We didn't even get past the fifth verse before I heard this blood-curdling scream from the women's section. Our demon-possessed woman came running down the hall screaming at the top of her lungs, "GET ME OUT OF HERE!!!" She ran right past me at the front desk and kept on going—out the front door and she has never returned. She did not pack any bags; she just ran, and we have never seen her since.

Walter never did call me back. A couple of years later I mentioned to him: "Walter, when I was first starting out at the Mission, you did me the greatest favor. You were so helpful to me."

Walter looked at me for a few seconds and said, "What did I do?"

"We had this crazy lady here, and I didn't have a clue how to deal with her, so I called you."

More pause.

"You didn't answer your phone, and you didn't call me back."

Walter's expression changed to a look like he had just been insulted.

"No, you don't understand. That was exactly what I needed. When I couldn't reach you, and I didn't know what else to do, I just started praying and listening. That is all I do now. I pray and listen, and God tells me what to do."

CHAPTER 12

FREEDOM HOUSE

THE DISCUSSION IN OUR BOARD meeting for May of 2002 turned to the overcrowding at the Rescue Mission and the need to expand. Even though we didn't have enough money for the project, the Board needed to know a ballpark price, so they authorized me to hire an architect and begin the planning of how best to expand the Mission to accommodate more people.

The next morning, before I could start contacting architects, Hance McKinney was calling.

"Blake?"

"Yes."

"This is Hance McKinney. I want you to buy my property next to the Mission."

"Well, I had not thought about that before. How much do you want for it?"

"Five hundred thousand dollars."

Hance McKinney never was one to beat around the bush. He went on to explain that he was retiring and moving to Fredericksburg. He was one of five partners who owned the tract of a little more than two acres just south of the Rescue Mission. The exact percentage of each partner's ownership interest would rise and fall with the results of late night poker games.

That afternoon Mr. McKinney was at my office showing me the old plats outlining the property boundaries and all of the buildings on them. The tract was once combined with the land that the Mission was occupying to house the Texas Cotton Seed Oil Company.

Most of the buildings were constructed around 1910. The square-footage of each of the buildings was marked on the plat. I pulled out my calculator and added it all up—a total of 54,000 square feet of building space.

After studying the plat and hearing some history lessons from Mr. McKinney, he grabbed his ring of keys and we took a hike.

The first building we came to particularly caught my attention. It was a three story brick building at the entrance to the property which used to serve as the main office for the cotton seed operation. It was the smallest of the buildings at 4200 square feet, but, contrary to the other structures, this one could be renovated for housing with very little work. The first floor had a small apartment and a storage area. I knew that an artist had lived on the second floor with his wife and one child about three years earlier. It had been empty since then. The electricity had been turned off, but plenty of light beamed through the windows. It had a large living room and kitchen with two bedrooms, a bathroom, and a laundry room. The kitchen was twice the size of mine at home, and the bedrooms were spacious enough for two or three bunk beds in each room. The bedrooms had closets, too! The bathroom was big enough to accommodate three or four people at once without getting too cozy.

We started up the stairs to the third floor. The stairwell had no windows. We had to feel the wall and take careful steps as we navigated our way through the darkness to the third floor. From all of the trash that had been left behind on the second floor, I could not presume that the next step would be clear. Fortunately, Mr. McKinney remembered about where the stairway turned to the left. A strong push against the door on the third floor let some sunlight into the stairwell and sent the pigeons flying who had come in through the broken windows to roost.

Mr. McKinney bellowed, "They don't pay any rent; they need to go. Watch out for what they left behind. The fresh spots can be slippery."

Fortunately, the flooring on the third level was concrete. The second floor was hardwood. It desperately needed refinishing, but it had potential for something beautiful. Pigeon droppings really would have made a mess of that, but the concrete on the third floor could be easily cleaned. The third floor had a single bedroom and a huge living area which could hold seven bunk beds, at least two couches, and a television. The best feature was a huge skylight which faced north, as if the third floor had been designed as an artist's studio. I saw huge potential beyond the pigeon poop.

By comparison to the old men's dorm, the space available was cavernous. My immediate thought was that we could move all of the men who sign up for the Relapse Prevention Program into this building. As an instant reward for their constructive decision to enter the program, they would receive a significantly more spacious place to live.

The Relapse Prevention Program is the Mission's 13-week drug and alcohol recovery program. While the course covers the psychological and sociological aspects of addiction, the central focus is on the Gospel. As the people study God's word and invite the Holy Spirit to take control of their lives, the Holy Spirit then empowers the believers to overcome the temptations of their addictions.

All of the men participating in our Relapse Prevention Program had been living in the men's dorm. Picture 95 beds in a space of 2400 square feet. I knew that the situation was problematic because we had men who were trying to escape from a life of drugs and alcohol who might be sleeping in a bed next to someone who had just hopped off the train, had little interest in sobriety, and might be carrying temptations in his pocket. I knew that we needed to move our program participants to a space where they would be confronted with fewer temptations, but we simply had no place to put them.

There were five buildings on the property plus an 80-foot tall concrete structure holding fifteen grain silos. I couldn't immediately think of a purpose for that one. All of the other buildings were constructed for industrial uses and would need extensive remodeling to become anything else. The walls and floors were made of concrete and were one foot thick. But four of the buildings had rent-paying tenants in at least part of the buildings, and the total of all of the rents came to $4500 per month. I saw the vast potential.

After the tour I returned to my office and pulled out the calculator. I looked up the property on the tax rolls for the amount of real estate tax paid each year and did a revenue-expense calculation using percentages that I felt we could obtain on bank loans. Then I prayed about what number we should offer. Even though it seemed low, the number of $375,000 stuck in my head.

I saw the potential for housing the men in the drug and alcohol program in a separate building. Although that plan was not what I had in mind when I discussed the issues with our Board, I knew that new construction of four to five thousand square feet of additional space would exceed the price that I was now looking at to buy this entire tract.

I crunched the numbers and saw that if we were able to obtain the financing that I expected, the rental revenue would exceed the loan payments and expenses by almost one thousand dollars per month. It was a real estate no-brainer.

Our Board officers agreed with my reasoning, and I drew up an earnest money contract with the total offer price of $375,000. I called Mr. McKinney and told him that I would be submitting a contract, so he wouldn't be looking too hard for another buyer. He wanted to know our number, but I explained that I needed to talk with bankers, building inspectors, and our Board before finalizing papers. He was somewhat understanding. I had thirty days before the next Board meeting to get all the details in place.

My first call was to my personal banker who had handled my lawyer's business account. I had also moved the Rescue Mission's account to his bank shortly after starting at the Mission. I couldn't contain the excitement in my voice as I described the massive amount of potential and eagerly invited him for a tour at his earliest opportunity.

My enthusiasm was enough to get him away from stacks of loan documents and out into the El Paso sunshine. We started in my office looking at the plat and then took on the physical inspection. All of the buildings except the brick one at the entrance were adorned in unfinished concrete. After 90+ years, they had begun to wear a bit. Mr. McKinney had explained to me how water seeps into the concrete when we do get some rainfall. When the rebar inside the concrete gets wet, it rusts and expands which flakes off the outer portion of the concrete wall. Of course, every now and then a chunk of concrete the size of a softball would break off and come crashing down some forty feet to the ground.

I explained to our banker how the buildings were still very sound in spite of the flaking concrete, but that it may not be a great idea to spend a lot of time standing next to one of the exterior walls. As we walked through the property, I continued excitedly describing how this particular building could be turned into housing and that building could be rented out to cover the mortgage payments. At some point between describing the potential for different buildings, I turned and looked at his face. Instead of looking at potential, he saw the chunks of concrete that had fallen on the ground, the dull gray concrete walls with a few inches missing, and the almost century-old square rebar rods exposed. He didn't say a word, but his face shouted, "I don't ever want to repossess this!"

I could see that a more extensive tour would not be beneficial, so I cut it short. He thanked me for the tour and then politely said, "I am afraid this is not the type of project that our bank would be interested in funding."

I started calling other bankers, but now I was getting declined before I could even get them to look at the property. Meanwhile, one of the bankers, who was a donor to the Mission, suggested that I call a certain individual at another bank. To my surprise, he was receptive to the deal, but he stressed how we needed to process the loan very quickly. He never even asked to look at the property or at the plat. His bank was willing to finance only $250,000, or two-thirds of the purchase price, even though it had appraised for $530,000. Fortunately, I talked Hance McKinney into carrying a $75,000 note, and he was willing to subordinate his lien to the bank's. Still, we had to come up with $50,000 cash at the closing. I had a great sense of peace that this purchase was in God's plan for the Mission, but I had no idea where the $50,000 would come from.

Our next Board meeting went surprisingly smoothly. The Board authorized the purchase including the bank loan and the secondary note for $75,000. I had already prepared the earnest money contract, so I hand-delivered it to Mr. McKinney that afternoon. Three days later he called to tell me that his partners had approved our contract as written. One of his partners attended church with me every Sunday. I informed him the next Sunday how wise he was not to give God a counter-offer.

About a week later I overheard a conversation coming from our business office. Our chaplain asked, "Where is Blake getting the money for this down payment? Do we have $50,000?"

Jackie was our business manager. When she got really flustered, her voice would rise in both pitch and volume. "Fifty Thousand Dollars! We don't even have fifty thousand cents! He's nuts I tell you; he's just nuts; he's nuts!"

The next week Glen Pickett, our Board president, called to tell me that the Pilot Club had a little presentation to make and wanted me to schedule a special chapel service for that purpose. I felt compelled to say something inspirational, so I asked about the history of the Pilot Club. I was amazed at the similarities with some of the purposes of the Rescue Mission. Nell Gardner had formed the Pilot Home in El Paso to provide a place where elderly people with little means could reside and be treated with dignity and respect. When she was in her eighties, the home was taken through eminent domain so that Jefferson High School could expand. Not afraid to start over from scratch at such an age, Nell Gardner took the proceeds from the sale and immediately began construction on a new and improved Pilot Home. The Pilot Club was a group who wanted to carry on Nell Gardner's vision many years after her death.

With such information my inspirational speech was easy to prepare. Nell Gardner had found meaning in life by devoting all of her energies to helping others who were in desperate shape and had no means of caring for themselves, and, in doing so, God gave her greater energy to keep going and start over even after the government had torn down her accomplishments and evicted her tenants.

The chapel service was very well attended. Many of our homeless guests came along with some of our Board members and members of the Pilot Club. After a couple of songs and my speech, the members of the Pilot Club came to the front of the chapel for the presentation of a check to assist with the purchase of the new property. They handed it to me in a closed envelope. I opened the envelope and studied the paper inside for a few seconds. My eyes got a bit blurry as I struggled to count the number of zeros. It was for $50,000—the largest check the Mission had ever received in its fifty-year history.

I knew that the purchase was God's will, so I knew that God would provide, although I had no idea how that provision would take shape. I suspected the Pilot Club was coming to give us a check to help with the purchase, but I anticipated maybe five or ten thousand dollars from this group. I stood holding the check and struggling to hold back the tears. I tried really hard to say something but nothing would come out of my mouth. Glen Pickett said it was the first time he had ever seen me completely speechless.

When some of our guests heard that the brick building was to house men who were going through our Relapse Prevention Program, they came up with the name "Freedom House" and cut the name into a large board that was then fastened to the wall outside the building.

A month after the closing I called our friendly bank officer to thank him for believing in us, but I discovered that he had accepted an offer to become a vice-president at another bank. Then I realized why he stressed that the deal had to be done right away. He had pushed our loan through knowing that he was about to submit his resignation and would not be around to answer for it. I was beginning to learn how God manipulates finances.

After a few months we saw that our success rate in the Relapse Prevention Program had doubled since opening Freedom House. The men formed tighter support groups, and they were separated from the population that was not pursuing recovery. In a typical year we receive forty to forty-five people into the RP Program. Almost all of them meet HUD's definition of chronically homeless, and all of them have long-term drug or alcohol addictions. At least 30 of those precious souls graduate each year after having completed thirteen weeks clean and sober.

CHAPTER 13

JOHN

JOHN CAME TO THE MISSION in 1999. One of our Mission volunteers told me that John had been living in a cardboard box behind his small, rented house in Fabens. While a box is sturdy enough for most days that we have in El Paso, a sudden rainstorm had washed John's house into a muddy ditch. The volunteer had provided a garden hose and a towel and was coming to me to ask about clothes that might be John's size. I gathered up some clothing but insisted on driving out to Fabens myself. I wanted to meet John and invite him to come to the Mission.

John was grateful for the clothes and a little reluctant to leave the shade of his tree, but his home had collapsed, lying in a ditch half covered in mud. In fact, with very little vegetation in the field where he was staying, I couldn't take ten steps off the road in any direction without getting my shoes submerged in the mud. Once I described the meal we served the night before and told him that several more meals of equal quality were coming, John was ready to go. We knocked most of the mud off our shoes and got in the truck.

After a few days at the Mission, John learned about the next session of the Relapse Prevention Program which was scheduled to start in another week, and he was ready to sign up. We got to talking much more in the weeks to come. I learned that John had been a CPA, but the pressures of that work along with a history of failed relationships had driven him to the bottle. He lost his job and then everything else that had defined his identity.

At the end of the RP Program, John aced the final exam. One of our counselors expressed the concern that his answers were a little too perfect. He could remember every point made in every discussion, and he memorized the Overcomer's Twelve Steps down to the placement of each comma, but the counselor felt that the answers stopped at his brain and never reached down to his heart. He kept his shield up and didn't allow himself to be vulnerable.

John went to work at the front desk of the Mission answering phones, greeting new guests, and troubleshooting many of the problems that our guests dumped at the front desk. We had struggled for years to find someone whose personality provided the introduction we wanted to convey to someone coming into the Mission, and John was the perfect fit. At the same time, I knew that he was not being challenged and lived with a sense of shame at his vocational failure.

Four years later when our bookkeeper announced that she was resigning to take a job with better benefits, I started passing the word through other nonprofit agencies that the Rescue Mission needed a person to keep the books, process payroll, and pay the bills. I had thought about John, but I also knew that he was fragile and that work pressure had driven him to the bottle in the past. I didn't say anything to John about the job, and he didn't mention it to me even though I walked past the front desk at least twenty times each day.

About a month into my search, one of my staff members mentioned to me that John really wanted the job but that he was afraid to raise the subject directly to me.

I sat down with John after his shift, and we talked about how he was dealing with stress and whether he really wanted additional responsibilities. John acknowledged his own concerns about falling back into drink, but he knew that this opportunity was his time to move from being a receptionist to doing the work he had been trained to do. I sure couldn't argue with his qualifications. How many other missions of our size had a CPA in their business office?

Of course, there were many times when we didn't have enough money to clear payroll at the end of the week; there was nothing in reserves, and businesses would be calling John demanding to know when their bills would be paid. The job was not without pressure. There had always been a healthy tension between myself and our previous bookkeeper. I tended to focus on ways we needed to expand to reach more needs. As long as I could still see needs, I was trying to figure out how the Mission could meet those needs. Our bookkeeper, meanwhile, was trying to figure out how to pay the bills from the last time that I had tried to meet more needs. One of her favorite sayings was, "It may be in the budget, but it's not in the bank!"

Once John was in her chair, I would hesitate a little before saying we needed money for some new service that I had thought up and, instead, put a little more thought into how to pay for it before introducing the idea to John. On rare occasions, we saw a few signs that John had slipped, but, for the most part, he handled the pressure, gave the bill collectors a calm assurance that they would be paid, and didn't resort to the bottle.

My only complaint was that John was too exacting. I was much more of a generalist. While John was writing down every penny, I kept the numbers in my head. I knew how much we needed by the end of the week to clear payroll and pay the electric company and other pressing bills. I had a general idea of our bank account balance, and I knew how many checks I had signed yesterday which were being mailed out today. About an hour after the mail had arrived, I would call from my office and ask John how much we received in contributions through the mail. He was incapable of saying, "About $2400." Instead, the answer was, "Let me call you back." A few minutes later, my phone rang, and he provided the answer of "two thousand, three hundred, eighty-nine dollars and fifty cents."

After John had been in the business chair for about two years, I got a notice in the mail from HUD. In order to continue to receive money on a grant that I had written, one of our staff members was required to go to Fort Worth for the annual training session from the HUD office.

I went last year. I knew what to expect—a day and a half of the same information they told me the year before. I turned the pages in my calendar and saw how busy I would be with other things during that time. I didn't have time to drive to Fort Worth, and the airline was a pain.

Then I had a brainstorm—I would reward John for his good work by giving him an all-expense paid vacation to Fort Worth.

I went to his office to tell him how proud I was of his great accomplishments in his new job and that he had earned the right to represent the Mission at a very important meeting with HUD in Ft. Worth. He didn't seem too excited, but I told him that I would take care of his airfare, find him a nice hotel near the meeting and give him money for meals. Since John was still living in the Mission, I thought it was a great offer and would provide a welcome break for him.

The Texas regional office for HUD is in downtown Fort Worth, so they scheduled their meeting there and required all agencies serving the poor to attend, even though hotels in downtown Fort Worth tend to be some of the most expensive in the state. I did an Orbitz search for something somewhat affordable and booked John a room for only $125 a night about six blocks from the meeting. A few days before departure, I gave him his American Airlines ticket, directions for the Super Shuttle, $120 for meals and other expenses for two nights and wished him happy travels. To my surprise, he still didn't look too thrilled. The two-night trip, required by HUD so that we would be qualified to serve the poor, just cost us $750. Meanwhile, we were still struggling to find the money to pay for electricity and water for the month.

The morning after John's return, I went into his office to ask if HUD had any revolutionary news for us. John just leaned back in his chair with a slight smile on his face and sighed, "I made it."

I had not heard of any natural disasters in the area or airline strikes.

"You made what?"

"There were four bars between my hotel and the meeting. I had to walk past each one four times, but I made it." The expression on his face was one of half accomplishment and half exhaustion.

I had no idea what temptation I was throwing John into. He didn't want time away from the Mission. He didn't want a vacation, and I had sent him into temptation by himself that almost destroyed six years of sobriety.

At that point I realized that if John had set one foot inside one of those bars, he would have used all of the dining money I gave him for drinks, and, after one drink, he would not have stopped drinking until the bar closed down and they carried him out into the street. He would not have been able to find his way back to the hotel; he would have missed all of the HUD meetings; he would have missed his flight home, and he would have been left wandering the streets and alleys of Fort Worth in a drunken daze. By my offer of a vacation, I had come very close to killing him.

"Great job, John! I knew you could do it."

I have learned that some people cannot live in complete

independence, but they can do very well as long as they are in somewhat of a supervised environment. John was a prime example. As long as he was living at the Mission where he knew no alcohol was allowed, he could stay sober. He knew that others were watching him, and he had enough respect for the Mission not to attempt to bring a bottle onto the premises. He also had enough respect for me that he was determined to fulfill his mission of attending the HUD meetings without falling down. I could see in his face, however, that two days of walking past bars had pushed him to the limit, and I never asked him to go out of town again.

HUD has now adopted a one-step solution for everyone who is homeless called "housing first." The idea is to de-emphasize homeless shelters and, instead, put everyone into permanent housing as soon as possible, regardless of whether the people are willing to address the habits or addictions that caused their homelessness. The theory is that once a person receives adequate housing, the pressure is off, and the person will be more receptive to receiving rehabilitative services. But the offer of housing is not conditional upon participation in any rehabilitative program.

John stayed at the Mission and continued to work in the accounting office without missing a day for another three years. He continued living on the second floor of Freedom House where he served as a floor monitor for other men who had finished the classroom portion of the Relapse Prevention Program. He would assign chores and provide an available ear for others at Freedom House who might be struggling with thoughts of a relapse. When he was not working in the accounting office, he usually could be seen on the steps of Freedom House reading a book. Reading was both his recreation and his means of sharpening his mind.

I was more than a little surprised when John didn't come in for two straight days. My surprise turned to disappointed anxiety when one of my counselors told me that he sounded drunk when he called in sick.

"Drunk? In Freedom House?"

"No, he moved out a month ago."

Although he confided in me about most things, John had never mentioned that he was planning to move out of the Mission—or even that he wanted to move out. He had been living in a room with two bunk beds and plenty of space for hanging clothes and shelving his collection of books and movies. When the census rose, he had to share his room with others who had graduated from the Relapse Prevention Program, but he still had the nicest space that the Mission had to offer.

His move was all the more shocking considering how hesitant he had been to move into Freedom House. John had been living in the men's dormitory since he came to the Mission in 1999. In July of 2002 we bought Freedom House. We actually started to work remodeling Freedom House the day before our scheduled closing. My best informed guess is that the building was constructed about 1912 and had received very little renovation since that time. The kitchen did have some modern appliances, and the showers had been redone at some point, but the rest of the building was pretty close to the original. The hardwood flooring had to be sanded down and refinished. The plumbing for the sewer pipes was cast iron. All of the vertical pipes were in good condition, but wherever a pipe turned horizontal, allowing water to pool in it, the pipe had rusted through. Our first efforts at turning on the water revealed a dozen or more leaks.

All of the workers for the Freedom House renovation came from the Rescue Mission. Plumbers, sanders, painters, roofers, carpenters—all of the talents we needed were right there within the homeless population at the Mission. The only professional contractor we used was to pressure test the new gas lines before the gas could be turned on. By the middle of October, it was ready for occupancy.

I had the idea that we should announce an open house and invite all of our supporters. I chose the Saturday before Thanksgiving as the festive day to show it off and put the announcement in our monthly newsletter which was mailed out at the first of November. I had the thought that the building would show much better if we had at least one person living in it. John was still working at the front desk at the time and was living in our over-crowded men's dorm. At that time he had close to three years of sobriety under his belt.

"John, do I have a deal for you! I need someone to move into Freedom House before the grand opening, and you are the perfect choice. Take one of those bedrooms on the second floor, and you will have your own space until we fill up with RP students. Then, when we do get RP students moving in, you can be the monitor for the second floor."

John had been watching the construction in progress. He knew the new policy was for all Relapse Prevention participants to move to the large, open space on the third floor at the start of the thirteen week session and then the graduates could move to the second floor where they had more private space and a huge kitchen. My offer guaranteed John that he would have the entire second floor by himself for the next five months since all of the new students would be going to the third floor.

The next few weeks were busy with getting invitations out, coaxing the press into giving us some coverage, and planning out the food to be served when our guests arrived. Of course, an open house is the opportunity for donors to see what their money has done and to receive immediate feedback on what is happening at the Mission. We had made the purchase on faith with $375,000 that we did not have, so the appearance of the Mission had to make them feel good about the support they had given and inspire them to do more.

The Pilot Club had covered the down payment, and the closing costs had been rolled into the loan. We were left with debt payments and renovation costs.

A few days before the open house, I made a walk through inspection to be sure that everything was in perfect order. The floors had been refinished; all of the walls were painted; the molding was stripped and refinished; most of the plumbing was replaced; new gas lines were installed; new washers and dryers were placed in the two laundry rooms; a new furnace and water heater were installed, and all of the ductwork for the cooling units had been replaced. Then we had to furnish it with new beds and mattresses. Of course, I was paying our homeless workforce and buying all of the construction materials. The costs of renovation kept rising, and much of it was on my credit card, so we really needed to make a good impression with our donors.

I entered the second floor and went into the first bedroom. Everything was neat, but John's things were not there. I looked into the second bedroom, but he had not moved into that space either. Two weeks had passed since I told him to move. I went looking for John.

It was a little after four in the afternoon and John's shift had just ended. I found him sitting on a bench behind the Mission reading a book. There was a space on the bench next to him, so I sat down beside him.

"You didn't move into Freedom House."

"No."

"You know, we won't have any RP students moving onto the second floor until at least April. You could have that whole space to yourself with that big kitchen and bathroom."

"Yeah, I know. To tell you the truth, I'm a little scared."

"Of what?"

John put his book down and paused a moment.

"Well, things have been going really well for me just the way they are. The dorm is crowded and kind of noisy when the guy next to me snores, but I have been staying clean, and I am just afraid to change anything."

I leaned back on the bench and thought a bit about John's words. Once again, I caught myself trying to move someone at my pace instead of his.

"I tell you what, John. Just go make one of the beds, throw a pillow on it, and move some of your clothes and books over there so that it looks like someone is living there when the open house comes. You don't have to leave the men's dorm until you want to."

"Thanks."

John finally moved to Freedom House to join the rest of his things about two months later, but not before the next wave of RP students had already moved into the third floor.

Almost six years had passed since I had encouraged John's move into Freedom House. Reflecting upon that struggle, I was amazed that he had taken the leap to independent living without even discussing it with me.

It took a few days of asking around before I found a man who had helped him move and knew where he was. John had rented an efficiency apartment in a large complex. I drove to the apartment after work and knocked on the door. I saw John's van in the parking lot, but there was no answer, and no sounds were coming from inside.

The next morning I stopped by his apartment on my way to work, but, again, there was no answer to my knocking. John had now been gone from work for a full week. I asked about him at the apartment manager's office, but in the interest of preserving his privacy, they would not even verify if he lived there. After another day went by, I decided to call the police and ask for a welfare check. The police got the manager to open the door, and we found John passed out on his bed. There was a half-gallon jug of vodka on the floor by his bed with maybe an inch of liquid in the bottom. I found four more empty jugs in the bathroom.

With considerable effort we were able to get John up, and I asked his permission to dispose of the remaining vodka. I told him how important he was and how all of us wanted him to come back to work.

Two days later John came back to work, but all he could do was sit at his desk and shake. We finally persuaded him that a week at Trinity Detox would be a good move. He agreed to go if I agreed to come get him and take him back home whenever he asked. For most of the trip to the detox center he complained about how he had already paid rent for his apartment and was wasting money by not living in it.

After five days John called to say that he was ready to come home. I drove to the detox center to pick him up as I had promised. He was back at work the next day, and the next, but then the weekend came. We all held our breath and prayed for John that he would still be sober on Monday. Sadly, it was not to be. Monday came and went without John, and he didn't show up on Tuesday either.

When I mentioned to Darlene, our head counselor, that I would drive back to his apartment to pick him up, her response was:

"You're wasting your time, Boss. He's not finished."

I was revolted by her comment that my friend was somehow caught up in an alcoholic death spiral in which he was predestined to drink himself to the point of being "finished," knowing that several of my friends had died before they had "finished." The frustration was even greater knowing that Darlene had been right 100% of the time in perceiving when a person was ready to put the drugs and alcohol down and come clean.

Well, if I am powerless to prevent him from killing himself, at least I can try to stop him from killing someone else. I grabbed a friend living at the Mission who had an informal career as an automotive locksmith before he found Jesus. Within twenty minutes he had fashioned an appropriate tool from a piece of flatiron, and we drove to John's apartment.

John's van was parked outside. I parked my truck next to his van to provide a little bit of cover, and my locksmith went to work. Within five minutes the front door was open, and we popped the hood. I took my pliers and disconnected the battery. I had known John long enough to know that he was so non-mechanical that he would not even bother looking under the hood to spy the easy fix.

On Friday of that week, John called me for a ride to work. He was very apologetic about having missed the entire week and confessed that he had downed a few more gallons of vodka. He had run out on Wednesday and stumbled to his van to drive himself to the liquor store, but it wouldn't start. I confessed my criminal activity, and, to my surprise, he thanked me for caring.

Over the next four or five months, John might have worked thirty days. The end of our fiscal year was approaching, and we could no longer limp along trying to do John's work for him. The auditors would be coming for their annual examination of our books, and we had to have someone full-time. I painfully informed John that he was no longer employed.

Overlooking a few minor relapses, John had been clean for close to ten years. All but a month of that time had been spent at the Rescue Mission where he knew that alcohol was not allowed. Just the knowledge that he couldn't drink while at the Mission, and that people would be watching if he tried to drink was enough to keep him sober. But as soon as he had his own place and could live by his own rules, he sank quickly. I told him that his plan to move out might have worked if he had leased a two-bedroom apartment and found a roommate who would support his sobriety, but he didn't ask, and I stayed too busy to know that he was leaving.

Just as I had tried to move John along at my pace instead of his,

HUD's one-step, housing first solution for homelessness doesn't fit everyone's needs. For John, the shelter setting was healthier by far than having his own place. John's apartment had a television and VCR where he could watch his stacks of recorded movies and read books. He went home each day to isolation without any human interaction or supervision, and ten years of sobriety was destroyed in thirty days.

CHAPTER 14

RESCUE INDUSTRIES

WE CLOSED ON OUR REAL estate purchase of the old cotton seed oil refinery next to the Mission in July of 2002. By the next January, Freedom House was open for business with a new class of twelve homeless men who wanted freedom from the addictions that had taken control of their lives. While the property included over 50,000 square feet of industrial buildings with one-foot thick concrete walls, most of that space was rented out, and we were collecting $4500 per month in rent, while paying out $3500 in mortgage payments. The building I really wanted was Freedom House, which I knew could easily be renovated into housing for the men in our Relapse Prevention Program. The other buildings were suitable only for industrial purposes, but they were creating the revenue that paid the Mission to take over Freedom House.

What a deal! What could go wrong?

The biggest building was over 12,000 square feet and was leased to a furniture manufacturer for $2500 per month. Everything went well for the first few months. In November the tenant was late with his rent and paid up just a little before Thanksgiving. I already knew that December would be very late, but I held off from taking any actions with his assurances that nobody ever ordered any furniture at the end of the year and that his cash flow would improve in January. Besides, I had no hope of leasing the space to anyone else at the end of the year.

When I returned to work after the long Christmas weekend, I noticed that the far end of our new property was very quiet. I walked back there to see what was up and discovered that the furniture factory and all of its equipment were gone. My tenant had used the Christmas holiday to move out without any notice. I was now looking at a big, empty building and our real estate revenue just plunged below the amount of our expenses.

I called a few of my friends in the real estate business to see if they knew of anyone who would be interested in leasing such a large building. El Paso already had a long list of empty industrial buildings. I learned very quickly that I was not on the favorable side of the market.

After about three months we found a tenant who agreed to rent a portion of the building for $700 a month to warehouse computer parts, but we still had a very large empty space.

The next annual convention of the Association of Gospel Rescue Missions was in May of 2003 in Washington, D.C. Each year the association sets up a large exhibit hall for businesses to market their goods and services to rescue missions. A business could rent a booth and show its merchandise to every major rescue mission in the United States and Canada with one stop. One of the exhibitors was a furniture manufacturer from Virginia who was marketing wooden bunk beds.

When I started at the Mission, I had inherited almost 50 bunk beds made of angle iron. I was told that they were cast-offs from the military. After only a couple of months, one of the men from the dormitory told me that a bed had broken the previous night. I went to the dorm to inspect the bed and discovered that the piece of angle iron on the side of the upper bunk had suddenly cracked in two, depositing its resident on the floor.

We did not have any reports of any other beds rails cracking, so I dismissed it as a bizarre accident.

Then, a few months later another bed failed in exactly the same manner. Both cracked bed rails were on the upper bunk in the center. The side of the upper bunk quickly bent from a straight line to a V-shape. Fortunately, neither bed failure resulted in any permanent injuries, as the crack created such a sudden and severe slope that the mattress slid off of the upper bunk with its occupant, thereby creating a little cushion when both of them hit the floor. But now I was determined to replace all of the beds with something else before anyone was hurt. The personal injury lawyer in me demanded a very prompt change.

We had a few residents who had some carpentry skills, so I sketched out a design on a legal pad, bought the lumber, and put them to work constructing our first wooden bunk beds. We used pine four-by-fours for corner posts and two-by-six lumber for the side rails. I was determined that no one was going to be hurt because one of our beds broke.

The bed I was looking at from this exhibitor wasn't bad, but it wasn't as solid as the ones we had already made. I couldn't help myself from studying his bed and comparing the way it was built to the bunk bed I designed. Although his bed was built for standard twin mattresses, the space between the upper and lower made it a better fit for kids than adults. I couldn't sit up on the lower bunk without hitting my head on the upper. I thought our joints were stronger, too. The more that I looked at his bed, the more satisfaction

I felt about our accomplishment of filling our men's dormitory with our own bunk beds.

Then the light bulbs started going off in my brain. We have that great big, empty building that used to house a furniture factory. All of the heavy-duty electrical wiring is still there. I have hundreds of people coming through the Mission who are desperate for jobs, and there aren't enough job opportunities for them in El Paso. I had wood shop in 8th and 9th grade, and I made an "A" each semester. My bunk bed design is better than his. We can do this!

The crowd was already gathering for lunch as I was leaving the Exhibit Hall. My mind was racing ahead to the costs of production. Lunch was served in a huge banquet hall holding 80 round tables big enough for 10 chairs at each table. I looked around for the three other Mission employees who had come from El Paso, and we sat together. While the others started talking about the ideas they had heard presented in their morning seminars, I unfolded my paper napkin enough to make a writing surface and started figuring costs.

When I was designing the bunk beds, I never calculated exactly the material cost for each one. I knew what materials we needed to make a good, solid bed, and then we compared prices at Lowe's and Home Depot to get the best deal. I had bought enough lumber to have all of the numbers in my head. Each bed used two, twelve-foot four-by-fours which were cut in half to make the four corner posts. Each two-by-six side rail was six and one-half feet long. We needed four of them. The boards at the ends of the rails were 44 inches long, and we needed four of them. The head and foot boards were braced with two-by-fours. Each of those was also 44 inches long, and one bunk bed took six of them. Within a few minutes, I had all of the numbers on the napkin and knew the approximate cost of the wood going into each bunk bed.

I suddenly noticed that the conversations next to me had stopped, and my coworkers were staring at my napkin. Darlene looked at Juana and asked with a tone of apprehension, "What's Blake up to?"

I smiled at her and declared, "We are in the furniture business."

One of my best workers among our residents at the Mission was Scott. He would work with determination and enthusiasm until a job was finished, and he had a brilliant, mechanical mind. Scott had built most of the bunk beds that we were using.

When the transmission on one of our vans went out, Scott dived right into the task of fixing it. Within a couple of hours of my giving him permission to try, the van was jacked up, the transmission was out, and Scott was pulling out all of the parts. I never realized how many parts were in an automatic transmission, and there they all were—laid out on our parking lot in pools of old transmission oil.

Scott may have been energetic and a mechanical genius—at least by my lawyerly standards, but he was also bipolar. When life started going pretty well for him, he would reason that he really didn't need his medication any more. Then everything would explode.

We got the phone call from the Otero County Jail. Scott was a little vague on the details, but the story involved kicking out a window of a police car. At any rate, Scott would be living somewhere else for a while.

We collected a few boxes and gathered up all of the transmission parts from our parking lot, and I called a tow truck for the van. I was not really surprised to get the call from the mechanic a few days later telling me that several parts were missing.

My next thought, immediately after announcing to my crew that we were in the furniture business, was that it was about time for Scott to get out of jail.

At the end of the convention, I boarded the airplane, flew back to El Paso, and drove directly to the Mission. There was Scott sitting on the front steps. As soon as I got out of my car, he jumped up and ran toward me pleading, "Can I have my job back?"

"Yes, but I have an even bigger job for you. We are going into the furniture business. You are going to be our first teacher. We will have a 100% homeless workforce, and we will employ and teach job skills to as many people who are homeless as we possibly can. Then we are going to sell our products and advertise them as made by people who are homeless. Our first priority is to make jobs available, but the second goal is almost as important. Most people out there don't think homeless people can do anything productive. We are going to make first-class products that will be so impressive that our customers will say, 'Wow, I can't believe people who are homeless made this!' We are going to change the perception that society has of those who are homeless by showing off the quality of their work. Are you on board?"

"You bet! When do we start?"

"Now. Let's go create our new shop."

CHAPTER 15

WHERE WE CAME FROM

WE ALL LEARNED IN SCHOOL of the American "self-evident truth" that all men are created equal. I am not sure what was going through Thomas Jefferson's head when he penned those words. While he may have desired that all men should be treated equally under the law, there is no greater self-evident truth than that each of us started this life from very unequal positions.

Most people who are homeless will not tell you where they have come from until they get to know you very well. For most of them, their past is so difficult that they are afraid you would reject them if you knew their stories.

My usual reaction once I have learned where a person at the Mission came from is to doubt that I could have done any better if I had endured the same past. The stories of Casey, Richard, and Tammy are not unusual—unfortunately. They describe the massive obstacles they have had to overcome.

CASEY'S STORY

One of our state judges called me about Casey. He had been indicted for aggravated assault when he was 17. The judge had been watching the calendar and called me on Casey's 18th birthday. He told me that he didn't believe Casey really had a problem with violence. The real problem, the judge had concluded, was that Casey had no father and was living in a crack house with his mother. The judge gave me the address and asked if I would go visit Casey to see if he would like to come live at the Mission.

That afternoon I drove to the small apartment in northeast El Paso. From the looks of the place on the outside, it couldn't have been larger than 300 square feet and did not seem to have any air conditioning. After I knocked, Casey cracked the door open and stuck his head out.

"Hi, you must be Casey. Your judge asked me to come see you. I run the Rescue Mission of El Paso. It's a shelter for people who are homeless. The judge thought that the Mission might be a better place for you to live than where you are now."

Casey looked at me for about three seconds and then said, "Just a minute." He pulled his head back and closed the door. He was being careful not to let me see anything that was inside the apartment.

After a few minutes, Casey opened the door and came out holding a large plastic trash bag which he said contained all of his clothes. I put the bag in the back seat of the car, and Casey got in.

We had about a twenty-minute drive back to the Mission, which started out awkwardly quiet. Casey just sat in the car and didn't say anything. After a couple of miles I started telling him about some of the things the Mission had to offer, our food service, and the arrangements I had made for where he would be living.

He still had no questions about where he was going, so I asked him about his school. Apparently whatever was going on in his family had prevented him from meeting the attendance requirements and he dropped out. I told him that we could help him get to school if he wanted his high school diploma and that I would help with the expenses. He started to sound a little relieved.

Casey adjusted quickly to the new Mission setting and seemed very grateful to be there, although he had difficulty understanding why he should be subject to a 10:00 p.m. curfew now that he had turned 18.

Casey never told me what was going on inside of that little apartment that he didn't want me to look into, and I didn't ask.

About three months later Casey came into my office and said, "Here, I need you to hold this for me."

Casey held out a Visa Card. It had his name written on the front of the card.

I have had a lot of homeless people hand me things to keep for them, but I have never had anyone give me their credit card.

"OK, I give up. What is the story behind the card?"

"After I turned 18, a credit card company sent an application to the old apartment. My mother filled it out, forged my name to it, and got this card. Then she took a $1000 cash advance to buy crack and left me with the bill."

RICHARD'S STORY

Richard said his earliest memory was of his mother leaving him in a corner on the floor of a casino while she went to work. Several years later he realized the nature of the work. His father could have been any one of hundreds of her customers.

When he was four years old, the state of Arizona took him away from his mother and placed him in a foster home. But the foster family was actually worse. They burned him, broke his legs and his nose, and fed him only white rice, while the others enjoyed a full meal.

When he was 12, in a desperate search for a real family, he joined a gang, started carrying a gun, and sold drugs. He tried to play football when he started high school. Just before a game started, some team members ganged up on him and stuffed him in a locker where he was imprisoned until the end of the game. As soon as the opportunity arose, he retaliated by stabbing the varsity quarterback with a knife, and his formal high school education came to an abrupt end.

When he was 17, one of his drug deals went badly. His customer tried to rob him, so Richard shot him twice through the neck. He wound up spending the next four years in the Arizona penal system. When he was released, he met Jamie (the same very talented young lady in the chapter "Be My Friend."). The two of them decided to come to El Paso to visit Jamie's sister. While they were here, they thought burglarizing a liquor store would be a good means of raising some money.

Both Richard and Jamie went to jail but were eventually released on probation. They were no longer welcome at Jamie's sister's house, but one of the conditions of probation was that they could not leave El Paso, so they were homeless. After a few days they found their way to the Rescue Mission.

Richard was energetic, helpful, and had an eagerness to learn new things, so I hired him to work in our wood shop, and there he met Jesus.

Some of our workers would bring radios with them to listen to music while they worked. Most of our workers are graduates of our Relapse Prevention Program, where they learned to rely on Jesus and were taught that God's Holy Spirit within them would give them the strength to overcome temptation. Of course, we needed a policy of music control. Different radios blaring different songs at the same time would produce a cacophony where no one could work, and we needed to support our children in recovery by barring the destructive influences of some secular stations. So the policy was very simple. You can listen to K-Love, or you can turn it off and sing to yourself.

After a few months of listening to K-Love at least seven hours a day, Richard heard a lady giving her testimony on the radio. It touched him deeply, and he surrendered to Jesus.

Immediately upon receiving Jesus, the anger and bitterness that had possessed him was gone. Also, he suddenly became trustworthy. I could hand him my credit card and tell him to go buy building supplies with perfect confidence that my instructions would be followed and that he would find me the best deal he could. As John wrote in his Gospel, "To all who did receive him [Jesus], to those who believed in his name, he gave the right to become children of God." (John 1:12 *NIV*) Richard's transformation into a child of God was immediate and very apparent for everyone to see.

One Sunday morning I was sitting in church next to Richard. The pastor was preaching out of the New Testament but made several references to Abraham. Richard leaned over and whispered in my ear, "Who is Abraham?"

For those of us who have been raised in the church, it is hard to imagine the lack of knowledge of the person who has never heard anything at all about the Bible.

God had prodded me for several months with the idea of starting a discipleship group for new believers. I had delayed starting the group because the task of re-parenting someone like Richard seemed a little overwhelming, and I didn't know where to start. He is a 24-year old man who never had a real mother or father to provide direction. How many times are we so unsure of where to begin that we never begin at all? Our fear of not taking the perfectly correct first step leaves us afraid to move. God's clear answer is, "Just start."

TAMMY'S STORY

Tammy's mother ran away when she was very young leaving her father, an older brother, and two sisters in the house. Her father taught her how to make him money through prostitution. Her older brother was a drug runner. When she was nine years old, her brother was afraid she would squeal on him, so he held her down and shot her up with heroin.

Once the needle was out, he looked her in the eye and said, "There, now you can't talk. You're a junkie just like us." Her father stayed too drunk to know what was going on with her at the time.

For the next thirty-five years Tammy lived a life of prostitution and drugs until the trucker she was riding with drove off and left her in El Paso.

She started the Relapse Prevention Program four times before finally completing the thirteen-week program. Each time the topic of discussion hit on a particularly raw nerve, or when a personality conflict arose that she could not resolve, she responded by running away. She would go to the truck stop, hitch a ride to wherever, and let the cycle begin again.

However, this time she knew there was some place she could go where people would care for her. Each time she ran away, she would find more abuse and call me for a bus ticket back to El Paso, and each time she ran, the abuse got worse.

I remember taking her to church with me. We were singing a song about how Jesus forgave all our sins and has thrown our sins away as far as the east is from the west. She began crying hysterically, and there were not enough tissues in the pew.

She has now been clean and sober for almost two years, and she has begun a program through one of our courts of mentoring young prostitutes to show them where the lifestyle leads and how to escape.

There were times while shelling out the money for four different bus tickets to bring her back to a safe place that I was questioning whether I was wasting my money. Now I feel like those payments were some of the finest investments I have ever made.

I am often asked how many successes we have. The inquiry begs the question of "what is success?" Most of us tend to think in terms of events that symbolize a great accomplishment: graduation, getting a job, getting a place to live, making a sale, getting a promotion. Working at the Mission has taught me to take more time to understand where the people came from and then join them in celebrating each little step of progress. Maybe success is just one more day of sobriety or not responding in a violent manner when encountering a personality conflict.

Tammy's graduation from the RP Program was a great success. But it was also success when she reentered the RP Program and completed for four weeks before quitting, whereas the last time around she quit and ran away after only two weeks. It was a success when she realized that she made a mistake by leaving the Mission and catching a ride with a trucker whom she did not know, and it was a success when she called me from a hospital bed asking for another bus ticket back to the Rescue Mission. She finally made it through the thirteen-week program. It took her two years of little successes to get there.

CHAPTER 16

ALL YOU NEED TO KNOW IS RIGHT THERE IN SCRIPTURE

OUR SHOP HAD A BIG furniture order from another mission—bunk beds, chests of drawers, bedside tables, and armoires. The order would fill a 52-foot trailer. The only problem was that I had informed the customer that it would be ready last month! I had calculated how long it should take us to manufacture each piece, and it was taking twice as long. The additional time translated into increased labor costs, which translated into red ink instead of black.

I had to call the customer again and explain why shipment would be delayed for at least another two weeks. I was sitting at my desk trying to think of another excuse when Harold came into my office.

"What's the matter, Boss? You look a little down."

"Harold, I know we can do this work, but I just can't seem to get the crew in the shop motivated to crank it out. We fall farther behind every day."

"Well, Boss, all you need to know is right there in scripture."

I leaned back in my chair and stared at him for a few seconds. "Harold, what are you talking about? I don't remember anything in scripture that tells me how to run a furniture factory."

"Sure there is! 'Whatsoever ye do, do it heartily, as to the Lord, and not unto men.' What would happen if everyone worked like they were really working for Jesus?"

I recognized the passage from Paul's writings, but frankly, I did not remember exactly where it was. I had to look it up in my Concordance.

Harold was quoting from the third chapter of Colossians. I read over the section several times about how servants are to do their work as if they were working directly for Jesus instead of for men. Then I backed up and read the whole third chapter of Colossians. The chapter starts off about focusing on spiritual things and putting away sinful desires, since as believers in Jesus, we have been risen with Christ and share his heavenly nature. Paul then wrote about how to treat each other and how to structure our families. The chapter concludes with how to do our work.

As I read over the teachings in this short chapter, the thought struck me that if a person really lived two-thirds of the lessons contained in the chapter, absent severe physical or mental disability, that person could not remain homeless.

I called a meeting of all of our factory workers the next day, and we studied the third chapter of Colossians together. I told them that I may sign their paychecks, and "Rescue Mission of El Paso" may be printed on their checks, but they did not work for me, and they did not work for the Mission. "All of the work we do here is for Jesus. You are working for Jesus, and at the end of each day, you need to ask Jesus if your work has been pleasing to him."

I was the seminary graduate, but I had been focusing on all of the problems instead of on God's message. God sent a man who was homeless to remind me and all of our other workers that all of our work needed to be done as if we were working directly for Jesus.

Our big order was on the truck the next week.

CHAPTER 17

COACH KAISER

AFTER I WAS HIRED TO direct the Mission, I was praying about what I needed to be doing and how to reach the people there. The thought occurred to me that the people coming into the Mission didn't become homeless overnight. They had numerous problems which contributed to their being homeless, and I shouldn't expect those problems to be resolved overnight. Then I had the thought that if I were able to assist in improving the lives of one or two percent of the people coming into the Mission, would that small percentage be worth my efforts? Immediately my thought was, "Of course it would," and I set out to try to reach the one or two percent.

After sixteen years I think the number whose lives have been meaningfully changed is closer to 20%, so I am thrilled at the work God has done, and I am humbled to be a part of it.

One of my favorite parables is the sower of the seeds. Before I started working at the Mission, I thought the parable was a bit silly.

I love planting a garden and caring for it as the plants grow. Any gardener knows that you spend most of your time preparing the soil, and then you carefully place each seed where you want the plant to grow. But Jesus told about a gardener who grabbed a handful of seeds and just threw them to the wind. Who would sow seeds that way? Some of the seeds fell on the road; some fell on rocky soil; some fell into the thorny weeds, and then some fell into good soil. Of course, we don't know what the exact percentages of each category were, but it sounds like the gardener in Jesus' story was successful with only 25% of his seeds.

I have learned that my job is to throw the seeds into the air. That way I make the opportunity available to all. My job is not to prepare the soil because, in spiritual terms, I don't know what good soil looks like. It is the job of the Holy Spirit to make each seed grow. I shouldn't try to do God's job. I just keep throwing seeds into the air.

As an obedient seed thrower, I am constantly amazed at which seeds grow and which do not. Sometimes a seed I threw in the air several years before starts to sprout long after I had given up on it. It is a good thing that God is in control of these things instead of me. So if the sower in Jesus' story was batting .250, my .200 average is looking pretty good.

I never know which seed will sprout, but what a joy to watch the growth that God brings! Mark Kaiser's story is one of joyful seed growth. The original seed was planted by a persistent lady in Las Vegas who never knew whether the seed sprouted or not.

Mark had been a heroin addict for over ten years. His home was a refrigerator box under a bridge in Las Vegas. He would eat out of dumpsters and beg on the street corners for enough money for another shot of heroin.

His life was so miserable that he would cry out to God at night just to let him die. Every now and then he would give himself an extra shot of heroin in the hopes that it would put him over the edge, and he would be out of his misery.

A lady stopped in front of him as he was panhandling on a street corner and handed him a bag of pretzels and a five-dollar bill. Then she started talking to him about how she had been in the same place where he was. She was on her way to her AA meeting and asked if Mark would get in her car and join her. She kept talking on and on about how she used to do drugs, but now she was free.

Mark kept looking up at the traffic light, waiting for it to change, so this lady would go away. The light stayed red, and this lady just kept telling him about her AA meeting.

Mark thought seriously about giving her back the $5 if she would just go away, but his thoughts raced to how much heroin that money would buy. She just kept on talking, and the light wouldn't change. It must have been at least five minutes that the light was stuck on red. He didn't want to give up the money, and he didn't feel like he could just turn around and walk away, so finally he said, "OK, if I go with you to this AA meeting, will you bring me back here to this corner and leave me alone?"

Mark didn't remember a lot of the things said at the AA meeting, but he was impressed with the number of people who said they had been where he was, and they were able to break free from their addictions.

True to her word, she brought him back to his street corner and drove away. Mark was able to buy another heroin hit with his panhandled money and then retreated to his cardboard box where he shot up and passed out.

The next few days were as usual, but the memory of that AA meeting haunted him. After about a week, Mark got out of his box, left all of his possessions for whoever wanted them, and walked six miles to a detox center.

After a week in detox he moved to a rescue mission where he found a copy of the Gospel of John.

"The way John wrote seemed so real to me," Mark told me. "It was like he was writing, 'This is what I saw, and this is what Jesus did. You can choose not to believe it if you don't want to, but I know what I saw.'"

Mark invited Jesus into his life, but he still needed to find a place where he could live away from the influence of those who were selling drugs to him. He had stayed a few days at the Rescue Mission of El Paso before he moved to Las Vegas and established his residence in a refrigerator box. He remembered El Paso as a safe place where he did not know any drug dealers. He stuck his thumb in the air and arrived here a few days later.

Mark walked into the Rescue Mission just a few days before our next Relapse Prevention Program was about to start up. He eagerly signed up. The Relapse Prevention Program was meeting in a room with some weight-lifting equipment which people had donated to the Mission. Most of it was in poor repair, but Mark was ready to put it to use and rebuild the body that heroin had torn apart. At the end of the thirteen weeks of classroom work, he was able to bench press 350 pounds.

I was astounded at the transformation when Mark showed me his "before" picture. It was a small identification card which was issued by the mental health authority in Las Vegas. He had long, stringy hair and had shriveled to 160 pounds which didn't leave much meat on his six-foot, one-inch frame. After several months of healthy, rescue mission food and regular exercise, he had built himself back up to 225 pounds. Considering that he was 53 years old and had been living in a refrigerator box for seven years, the rebuilding transformation was truly miraculous.

Mark started working in the Rescue Mission's furniture factory on the afternoon following his graduation ceremony. He was building oak furniture which would be used in other rescue missions around the country. He said that the best part about the work was the people he was working with. They had all been stuck in their addictions and thought there was no way out, but each of them had spent thirteen weeks in the program which included at least one hour per day of Bible study plus additional time of Bible reading in preparation for the next class. Whenever he felt tempted to fall back into drug use, he could find several sets of sympathetic ears to hear his frustrations.

A month after completing the program, Mark met Amalia in the Mission's kitchen. She had sustained an injury to her shoulder and was receiving worker's compensation benefits. She was able to work with one arm but not two. Since her employer did not have work for her with a one-arm restriction, they referred her to the Rescue Mission for one-armed work in our kitchen.

After a surprisingly short courtship, Mark announced that he was getting married. I will never forget the expression on Mark's face when he described to me his new family of Amalia's kids, and even a few grandkids, who immediately received him into their home and adopted him as Dad. He said his life was just like the conclusion of the book of Job in which all of the blessings of this life were restored to Job. Mark was surrounded by a family who loved him just as if he had been there for them all along. Every time he talked about his wife or his new family, his face would start to glow, and sometimes a little tear would appear in the side of his eye.

Mark continued to work at the Mission for almost a year, but the Mission was unable to offer health insurance benefits, and Mark knew the importance of insurance for his new-found family. He announced that he was leaving the Mission to work at a warehouse where the employer offered health insurance.

On his last day we gave him a farewell hug, and I didn't see him again for almost a year.

The first of the year is a great time for reflection, prayer, and planning. The idea stuck in my brain in January of 2013 that we needed a physical fitness component to our Relapse Prevention Program. It was such an obvious thought that I was kicking myself for not having thought of it earlier. Increasing a person's self-esteem is essential to staying clean from drugs, and exercise is a vital component to building self-esteem. We could increase our already fantastic success ratio by encouraging our participants to get into shape during the thirteen weeks that they were in class each day.

We still had almost the same collection of broken and worn weight equipment as when Mark went through the program. I could see that some of the equipment was never being used, and some of it was so broken that it might be dangerous to use. The first step would be to discard all the broken equipment and buy the things that we actually needed. However, far from being a physical-fitness expert myself, I wasn't even sure what that equipment was or where to get it, and I knew that even if I bought all new equipment and placed it in the RP meeting room, most of our program participants would not know how to use it or not be motivated to use it. I needed a trainer. Mark Kaiser instantly popped into my brain. Since Mark had been hooked on heroin, had found freedom in Jesus, and had rebuilt his body while well past 50, he would be the perfect trainer to connect with and motivate our younger RP students.

I first inquired at our business office for the last address and phone number when he had been working in the furniture factory. I called, but the number had been disconnected. I then walked to the shop and asked several people whom he had been close to if they had an address or a phone number. I collected three different phone numbers. Each one of them had been disconnected.

I was out of options. Mark would be the perfect trainer for our new program, but I had no means of finding him. So often it seems that the last resort that we come to is the place where we should have started in the beginning. All I had left to do was to pray. "God, we need Mark. You know where he is. Touch his heart and tell him to call."

I guess Mark was a little slow in listening because it took about three days for him to call. It was the first I had heard from him since he left the furniture factory.

The call came to Darlene, our head counselor. He said he didn't need anything and wasn't really sure why he was calling, he was just checking in to hear how everybody was doing.

Darlene immediately responded, "I know why you are calling. Blake has been trying to find you. What is your number?"

Within a day I had Mark on the phone and set up a meeting for the next Saturday morning. I shared God's vision for a fitness component to the Relapse Prevention Program, and he was hooked. Then we headed to the stores to find the appropriate fitness equipment. While waiting for service, we discussed a few business arrangements. Mark would be coming to the Mission at least three days a week. We needed to provide him with enough money to cover all of his gas and compensate him for his time. I added a few numbers in my head and offered him a job. Mark made no counterproposals. He was thrilled that the Mission needed him and felt like he was coming home.

Within another two weeks I had the opportunity to talk to Mark about the rest of his work. His warehouse boss was abusive, and his working hours on the night shift allowed him less than an hour each day of awake time to spend with his new wife.

"Didn't you tell me that you used to work construction before you started doing heroin?"

"Yes."

"Do you want to do it again?"

The Mission really needed some additional construction workers for the building expansion. We were more than doubling the size of the Mission by adding on a respite care unit and greatly expanding our space to house disabled persons and homeless families with children. I wanted to employ as many homeless persons as possible for the construction, but I needed some more knowledgeable workers to teach the others.

Within another week, Mark was a full-time employee. He would work with the construction crew and then take a break before lunch to go to our gym with the students in our Relapse Prevention Program.

He still finds it hard to believe that we pay him to go to the gym and coach others how to work out while telling them how he had been a heroin addict but that Jesus had given him freedom and restored him to a life better than what he had before he started using drugs. Almost two years of marriage had created a little band of loving just above his belt line. While he appreciated the affection, he was excited about getting back into shape.

The twelfth step of the Overcomer's Goals is: "We gratefully outreach by sharing the message of victory in Christ." For many of us this leap into evangelism is intimidating. Mark found it really easy once he started. All he had to say was, "I was a drug addict just like you. I gave my life, as pathetic as it was, to Jesus. Then God rebuilt me into what I am today. My health is restored. I have a home, and I have a big, beautiful family who all love me, and I love all of them, too. I love the work that I am doing, but the best part of my day is going home to my beautiful wife and watching the huge smile appear on her face as I walk through the door. I really do not understand why I am so blessed. I must be living the definition of the grace of God."

Mark Kaiser's ID card when he was in Las Vegas

Blake Barrow and Mark Kaiser on Graduation
Day from the Relapse Prevention Program

CHAPTER 18

T-BONES

I WAS READING THROUGH THE *El Paso Times* and spotted a sale advertisement from the Sun Harvest Grocery Store. They had T-bone steaks on sale for only $3.99 a pound. Wow! What a great price! My immediate thought was how nice it would be to bring my barbecue grill from home and grill T-bone steaks for the residents of the Mission. Some of them may never have had a nice steak in their whole lives.

I recalled the time that I had taken a trip to the Texas Gulf Coast and returned with some really fresh red snapper in my cooler, but I bought a few too many. After eating my fill for two days, I still had three nice snappers left over. I hated the thought of putting them in the freezer, so I packaged up the fish and some spices and took them down to the Mission. We had three workers who had really risen to the top in making the furniture factory work, and I wanted to reward them. I called each of them and told them to meet me at the kitchen at 6:00 p.m. and to come hungry.

I scaled and seasoned the snappers and put them in the Mission's oven on broil. I gently turned them after ten minutes to leave them slightly browned on both sides and then served them up on big plates to my guests. The smallest snapper was a pound and a half, and the largest was right at two pounds. No side dishes were necessary. I remember the sight of the faces of my guests as they dived in. The leader of our shop was Sam Casper. I gave him the largest fish. One of my guests had already finished his and began eyeing Sam's fish.

"That sure looks good," he said, looking at Sam's fish.

Sam pulled his plate closer and raised his fork in his fist with the tongs pointed at the table as if to stab any hand which moved too close. "This one is mine. Yours is over there," Sam proclaimed. He had the look of a rabid dog in his eyes. God have mercy on anyone who would have approached his fish at that time. I am certain he would have used his fork to harpoon any approaching hand.

Once they had removed all of the meat their forks would get, they picked up the skeletons and sucked on the bones to remove any last morsel including the little bit of fish juice left on the bone. Then each of them leaned back in their chairs with a look of complete satisfaction on their faces, rubbed their bellies and groaned a bit. A dozen ants would have starved trying to survive on the leftovers.

The experience of watching their absolute enjoyment by feasting on a treat which is never available in the desert Southwest was worth whatever I had paid for the fish. I had already experienced the delicate flavor and soft texture of the fresh snapper, so I was not tempted to join in on their portion. My satisfaction level was greater just by watching them savor it.

The enjoyment of cooking is the creation of a delight for the senses, but the pleasure of the creation goes only so far through self-enjoyment. To magnify the pleasure, the chef needs to share the creation and then watch the faces of others enjoying it also. Since I had already experienced perfection on the palate, the only way to enhance my personal pleasure was to share it with others whom I cared about.

I think the pleasure of sharing a fantastic meal is enhanced even further by sharing it with those who would never have had the capacity to obtain it themselves—either through purchase or preparation. Besides, a purchased meal is an entirely different experience. It is participation in a commercial enterprise and the enjoyment of your own success by being able to pay for the meal. On the other hand, when a person receives a meal as an undeserved or unexpected gift, the experience is completely different. The recipient knows that the preparer put money into the gift by purchasing the food and then devoted talent and labor into the preparation and service of the meal. It may be one of the best expressions of Christian love, and the person receiving the meal cannot mistake that motivation behind it.

I wonder if the people coming into the Rescue Mission feel like they are receiving a gift of Christian love when they get a meal? What are we saying to our homeless guests through our food? Most people coming into the Rescue Mission probably think the Mission receives USDA food from the food bank and maybe the government provides some funding for food service. The service of a bare-bones meal communicates that someone in government doesn't want them to starve, so this is what they get. Or, perhaps the thought is, "This meal is my entitlement as an American citizen, and someone is paying you to prepare it for me. The meal doesn't mean you care about me; it just means you are doing your job." Or worse yet, maybe the person is thinking, "I am a total failure in life, so this meal is what I deserve."

On the other hand, a meal that goes above and beyond is an unmistakable communication of Christ's love.

I have often pondered the thought of how much is enough, or, in the reverse, at what point is the meal too nice? After all, the Rescue Mission was giving the meals away, and, with a few exceptions, none of our guests were able to pay fair market value for it. Shouldn't our visitors be grateful for what they get? There is a huge difference, though, between being thankful for receiving your daily bread and receiving a meal that stimulates the response of "Wow, why are you being so nice to me?"

After giving the subject considerable, prayerful thought, I think I have an answer. Jesus told us in Matthew 25 that when we offered a meal to one of the least of his brothers in need, we were offering that meal directly to Jesus. So here is the standard: If we know, with a certainty, that serving the next person walking through the front door of the Rescue Mission is just like serving Jesus himself, and we invite Jesus into the dining room, would we be ashamed of the meal that we have to offer him? Then, at the end of the meal, did our actions make Jesus feel like an honored guest, or did Jesus feel like he had been a burden and we had an obligation to care for him?

Back to the T-bones. I did not feel like I could buy T-bone steaks out of the Mission's budget, which was already stretched to the point of praying for divine intervention to pay the regular bills. No, a T-bone purchase had to come from my own pocket. I examined my wallet, the checkbook balance, and thought about the bills that must be paid by the end of the week. I concluded that the most I could buy would be 50 16-oz steaks. I called Sun Harvest and ordered them up. At first the butcher protested that I was depleting his inventory, but when I told him it was for a special event at the Rescue Mission, he agreed to start slicing.

The next problem, of course, was that we had about 120 people staying at the Mission, not 50. Then I had a brainstorm. I didn't have to serve everyone! I could identify the people who were working to try to improve their lives and give them a steak as a reward, and, at the same time, I would be sending a message to those who were doing nothing to help themselves that more effort on their part would be a good thing. I even went so far as to tell our chef to tone down the regular meal for steak night. I wanted the contrast to be very well apparent. I wanted our guests to make the observation that the people who were always volunteering to help, or those who were earnestly looking for jobs, or those who were going to school to better themselves would get steak, while those who were not putting out the effort to improve themselves or their surroundings got bean soup. I told the chef to serve his toned-down meal first and then those invited for steak would eat later. That way, all of the people eating bean soup would see me behind the kitchen stoking the fire for steaks.

Not having performed such an experiment before, my mind raced ahead as to all of the problems I would encounter. I could identify the elect and give them an invitation, but when everyone stormed the pit for a steak, could I remember whom I had invited and whom I had not? I reasoned that the solution was to print tickets. Also, tickets would give me the opportunity to reinforce the message behind the meal. So I went to my computer and prepared a page of tickets—two columns, twelve tickets per page.

In appreciation for your hard work
to improve your life,
you are invited to a steak dinner with Blake
Wednesday evening at 6:00 p.m.
You must present this ticket to
receive your steak.

I printed up enough pages to cut out 50 tickets. Then, I thought, "these tickets would be too easy to put on a copy machine and counterfeit." So I took my blue ink pen and signed my name across the face of each one.

50 tickets; 50 steaks.

I set out on my journey to pass them out. The first stop was to the furniture factory where our 100% homeless workforce was crafting products that we would sell to other missions. They all got tickets. The next stop was to the men's dormitory where I found the men that I had seen cleaning the bathroom and mopping the floor. They all got tickets.

An announcement came over the loud speaker that we needed help unloading a truck at the back of the Mission. I watched to see who responded to the call for labor and then passed out more tickets.

My next stop was the medical rooms. There I found Sheila. She had been living in a homeless camp and had been attacked by a man with a knife—three deep slashes across the abdomen and another one at the base of the neck. The doctor told her that if the slash on the neck had been 1/8 of an inch deeper, she would no longer have been with us. She had four lines of metal staples holding herself together. The cuts were so fresh that she was still oozing a little fluid. I am sure she would have volunteered to help with the truck if she had been able. She got a ticket just for having the sense to leave the homeless camp and come to the Mission.

On my way out of the Mission, I saw one of our homeless guests hold the door open for a man in a wheelchair to pass. Both of them got tickets.

I asked my counselors how many people we had going to classes for their GEDs and wrote their names down on my search pad. I found them all, and each of them got a ticket.

I still had about ten left, so I just walked around the Mission watching the people. There were a number of men sitting on the back porch doing nothing, and another man was sweeping up cigarette butts off of the ground and putting them in the trash. He got a ticket. I made a point of giving him his ticket in front of those who were just sitting and watching.

By five o'clock Monday afternoon all but five of the tickets were gone. I still had a few to pass out Tuesday in case I missed someone who should have a ticket. I wanted to be sure most of the tickets were passed out well before the dinner so that the talk would go around as to who had a ticket and who didn't get one and why.

I fully expected to encounter a small mob of protesters Tuesday morning who hadn't gotten tickets and wanted some. I had my speech all prepared that the tickets were for people who had been helping out around the Mission. "But it's not too late to pitch in. If you want to wash dishes in the kitchen, you can have a ticket." The speech went unused as no one came to complain, so I made my rounds again in search of helpful residents and distributed the remaining five tickets.

On Wednesday afternoon I took the truck and trailer home to load up my 300-pound grill and towed it back to the Mission. I started the fire about 4:30 so that the coals would burn down to just the right level and I would be ready to throw on the steaks about 5:45. While the fire was getting started, our chef was sliding 50 Idaho potatoes into the oven. He prepared containers with sour cream, butter, chives and bacon bits; and I started seasoning the steaks.

The procedure was that those with tickets would file through the kitchen, select their potato, prepare it to their liking, and then bring their tray to the back porch to select their steak directly off the grill. I had the fire arranged hotter on the left than on the right so that each guest could select from the more well done steaks on the left to the rare ones on the right. Out of principle, I refused to cook any steak completely well done. As each person approached the grill, I would collect their ticket and then deposit the steak of their choosing on their tray.

Everything was going along very smoothly until Sheila approached the grill. She had her tray in one hand with her potato and her ticket in the other hand. As she walked up to the grill, I reached out for her ticket, and she pulled it back. She looked me in the eye and said, "Would you mind if I keep my ticket?"

Now that line certainly was not expected. "OK," I thought, "I will be watching for you when you come back through for a second steak."

"Sure, you can keep it. Which steak would you like? Rare is on this end, and well done is over there." She made her selection and moved on with a steak and her ticket.

Once all of the steaks were served, I had the opportunity to go into the dining room and watch my efforts being enjoyed. The expressions on the faces said it all. The meal was thoroughly satisfying, and nothing was left over.

To my amazement, not one person complained that he or she had been left out, and no one asked what needed to be done to be included in the next round of steak service. My motivational experiment had been a total failure. On the contrary, the people who did not get a steak figured that they didn't deserve one, and they were all right with that. My selective invitations probably had been counterproductive by confirming the negative self-esteem of those who already knew themselves to be failures.

The other surprise of the night was that I did not see Sheila again, and the number of tickets and steaks were in perfect balance. I was baffled as to what she had been up to.

About three months went by and I was walking into a chapel service. I was a little late, having plenty of other work to do, and one of the few available seats was next to Sheila. So I sat down just as our guest speaker started his message. He invited our guests to open their Bibles to a particular passage and follow along as he read the scripture. I had not brought my Bible with me so I looked over at Sheila and watched her as she opened her Bible. As she parted the covers, the pages fell open to a spot where she had placed a bookmark. It was a small piece of paper inviting her to a steak dinner, and it had my signature across the front of it.

I had to reach down for every bit of composure that I had to avoid crying in the middle of chapel. Even though she could not express it in words, her actions said, "No one has ever done anything this nice for me, and I want to hold onto this little piece of paper to remember this day." And I thought she was trying to steal an extra steak. I was so ashamed.

Another year later, I was talking with Richard Swartz on the back porch. Richard is one of the most creative people I have ever met. But his recurring alcoholism kept kicking him back into homelessness. For several years he had worked on making silver rings and pendants with his own unique designs. He wanted to show me his latest creation which he had just finished. It was a silver ring with what looked like various colored stones inlaid in stripes across the top of the ring. He pointed to a red stripe on the top of the ring that was about 1/8 inch wide by ½ inch long. "Do you know what this is?"

"No, but it catches the light very well."

"It is a Burmese Ruby."

"What is a Burmese Ruby?"

"Actually, it is a piece of a broken tail light that I found in our parking lot."

He had taken a piece of trash; saw value in it, and filed it down to the perfect shape to fit precisely into the space in the ring. I was impressed.

Then he pointed at an off-white stripe next to the red stripe. "And do you know what this one is?"

"No, I don't."

"That is a piece of bone from the T-bone steak that you gave me last year."

CHAPTER 19

RETHINKING FOODSERVICE

OVER FIVE YEARS AFTER THE T-bone experiment, I am still trying to understand the lessons these encounters presented. The group that did not get a steak did not get one because I, as the sole judge, could not perceive that they were doing anything to help themselves. To the contrary, I saw them just sitting around watching time pass. While I may have been trying to motivate them into some productive action, they did not perceive it that way. They were so sunk into feelings of hopelessness, despair, and failure that they knew that the mere act of asking would bring the deeper cut of additional rejection. Meanwhile, those who received a reward for their efforts were exceedingly grateful and remembered the event for years.

How do I get a person to move from the first group to the second?

Of course, the beginning point is to understand that I cannot make anyone move to the second group. They must move themselves—or at least they must have the desire to move.

Jesus asked Bartimaeus, "What do you want?" As we read the Gospel, it seems like such a stupid question. We have all heard the story so many times, and we know that Jesus was about to heal the man. But, what if Bartimaeus had answered, "I want money for a beer."

I will bet that some people actually did respond to Jesus in that manner, but such a story did not make it to the rough draft of any of the four gospels because not even Jesus would have performed a miracle in that setting.

What are the differences between Bartimaeus and group 1?

Bartimaeus recognized that Jesus had the power to give him a better life, and he believed that such a change was possible for him. He was dissatisfied with his life as a beggar, and when the very brief opportunity for change arose, he jumped up and grabbed it while ignoring the voices of others around him who were trying to put him down.

What character do we see in group 1? They might describe themselves with one of the following statements:

"I am a failure. I know that I am a failure, and I am OK with that."

Or, "I may not like being a failure, but that is what I am, and I can't change."

Or, "Change might be possible, but I have been defeated so many times that I don't know where to start."

What can I do to get a person out of the rut of despair, defeat, and depression?

I can redefine my concept of another's success. Each of the three categories describes a person who cannot lift himself out of his own failure. But the person in category one has no hope, while the person in category three has enough hope to be willing to take action, if shown where to start.

I can celebrate the success of a person acquiring hope, which is a necessary baby step toward success. Hope is the present awareness that we serve an active God who loves us and who intervenes in our lives and in the lives of those around us, shaping the future that God desires. We are not trapped in the rut of our future being nothing more than the natural progression from our past failures.

Robert was a skinny man in his late 30s with tattoos on his arms and legs. He had signed up for our Relapse Prevention Program. Some of the counselors suspected that he might be back on cocaine, so they demanded that he take a drug test. I gave him the little bottle and his instructions. A few minutes later he returned to my office holding his little bottle half-filled with fresh urine. I put the bottle on the corner of my desk and inserted the test card.

Robert sat down in the chair in front of my desk as we waited a minute for the results. I lifted the card from the bottle being careful to let all of the drips fall back into the bottle. "Congratulations, it is negative."

Robert's reply really shocked me. "Can I have the card?"

"You want the pee card?" I was trying not to let my surprise cause me to move my hand and have it drip on my desk.

"That would be the first negative drug test I have had since I was 12 years old."

Robert had been clean for a month. He was beginning to feel good enough about who he was that he didn't need to cloud his perceptions with cocaine.

Success was accomplishing 30 days without drugs for the first time in over 20 years.

Robert's recovery was rocky. He left the Mission before

completing the Relapse Prevention Program, and I don't know if he ever held a job long-term. By most of our standards, he did not approach success. Yet he did achieve 30 days clean for the first time in over 20 years, and I got to celebrate that success with him.

The Bible is full of examples of hope. Think of Joseph, who was sold into slavery by his own brothers, but he later discovered that slavery was the first step toward his becoming one of the most powerful men in the world.

How about the transformation of the disciples after Jesus died? They had given up everything to follow Jesus for three years. Not having grasped what he was really talking about concerning the Kingdom of God, their thoughts were, "Well, I just wasted a bunch of time. I guess I'll go fishing." Then Pentecost came, along with a complete understanding of what Jesus' ministry had been about.

Maybe if people see stories of hope developing in others, they might begin to realize that hope is possible, and they can start taking a few baby steps toward success. What can we do to proclaim more stories of hope to others in the Mission? How about printing an in-house Mission newspaper to publicize persons' accomplishments? When a person gets a job, we should celebrate with cake and ice cream after dinner and write up a story for other residents to read of how that person overcame his fear of the job interview. Then we need to encourage that person who has obtained employment to become a mentor for the others.

What else can I do to encourage a person toward positive change? The more I prayed about this question, I began to realize that many of our routine procedures were actually rewarding bad behavior. For over 60 years our Mission had been providing shelter and serving food free of charge to persons who were homeless. With limited exceptions, we required nothing in return. Residents were expected to pitch in to mop floors and keep the dormitory clean, but there was no structured system to determine who was avoiding cleaning opportunities.

I am frequently asked, "How long can a person stay at the Rescue Mission?" The party line has been the same for the 16 years that I have been the CEO, and all of our counselors know that response as well. The answer is, "I want to see that you are doing everything you can to help yourself. When you meet with a counselor, you and the counselor will make out a recovery plan which fits your individual situation, and as long as you are following that plan, you are welcome to stay." The reality, however, is that we have never had enough counselors to monitor whether each guest is following his or her recovery plan, and a person could easily lie around the Mission for 60 days doing pretty close to nothing before finally being asked to go do nothing somewhere else.

Ideas of requiring more contributions from our guests were accelerated by my own frustrations when the Mission encountered a time of extreme financial difficulties because so much money was going into the new building program. I would watch dozens of our guests walk up the hill to the Circle K and come back with a Big Gulp, a jumbo bag of chips, and a pack of cigarettes—easily spending ten dollars in one trip. Yet they were contributing nothing financially for their food and shelter. In effect, my actions were freeing up their resources to buy more cigarettes since I had food covered for them. I was enabling them to remain in their self-destructive lifestyles.

About the time I was entertaining these thoughts, I started reading Robert Lupton's book, *Compassion, Justice and the Christian Life*. He made the point that giving people something that they could have purchased themselves breeds entitlement, while intelligent giving to the poor empowers the poor to be able to care for themselves.

For a long time since working at the Mission, one of my favorite scriptures was Paul's admonition in 2 Thessalonians 3:10: "If anyone is not willing to work, then he is not to eat either." Note that Paul's last sentence in that paragraph is, "But as for you, brethren, do not grow weary of doing good." Paul was not contradicting Jesus' instruction to be generous to the poor, but he wanted the resources of the church to be directed toward those who were willing to work with their hands to help themselves and others.

We had a church youth group come to the Mission several years ago. I told them that flat surfaces were for the purpose of putting God's word before the people. Their task was to write scriptures on all of the walls. I didn't care what scriptures they used or where they put them, but this passage from 2 Thessalonians had to go above the entrance to the dining room.

The scripture had been on the wall for three years. I don't know how many people had read it, or what difference it had made in their lives. But I had not taken any further action to enforce it either. Time for a change.

I called a staff meeting to discuss the possibility of doing things differently for the first time in 60 years. It was not a meeting of "this is what we are going to do next." The tone was more of, "I have some thoughts. What do you think of this idea?" To my surprise, the staff was immediately and unanimously in favor of going to a system of requiring our guests either to pay for, or work for, their food.

We discussed some rules which would have to be in place with plenty of notice to our residents. My task was to write up the new rules to be placed on the dining room door announcing the policy change. My last statement to the group was, "Give me a starting date, and it can't be April 1."

We settled on the last Monday in March. I went to my office to write up the rules. By the time I finished writing, I was so excited about the changes that I went back and changed the start date to one week earlier.

Breakfast would be free—primarily because we did not have enough staff members on hand at that time to handle food service and the cash box at the same time. Lunch and dinner would be $1.50 per person, but all children would eat free, everyone too infirm to work would eat free, and anyone else who did not have $1.50 needed to see a counselor for a job assignment to work for his or her food. The counselor who assigned the job was then responsible for following up to ensure that the job had been performed satisfactorily. By putting the responsibility for follow up back on the counselor who issued the job instructions, I was trying to prevent too many jobs being provided to those who really had the capacity to pay. The counselor had to spend a little more time with the people to determine what their economic capacities really were.

I required our chefs to post the lunch or dinner menu on the wall by the entrance to the dining room at least three hours before serving time. I wanted the people to be able to see what they were expected to pay for. If they didn't like the menu selection, they were welcome to dine elsewhere. Like any other paying customer, now they could make their own decisions as to where they spent their money and plan accordingly. If a person were to decide that Burger King's menu was preferable to what the Mission was serving, then that person needed enough advance notice so that he or she could be prepared to travel to Burger King and back.

The next area of concern was with the kitchen staff. If we were going to start charging for food, even if the price was far below market value, the food had to be well worth the price. In the past our chefs had studied what had come through the door as donations, what would spoil if not eaten soon, or what had been in the freezer the longest, and designed a meal around what we had on hand. Actual food purchases were less than $5000 per year. I was proud of how our chefs made money stretch. How can you serve 700 meals a day, every day, for only $5000 per year? Sometimes, however, I thought we stretched the food budget a little too far.

My first thought was that everyone loves the smell of bread baking. I could not remember our chefs ever baking bread. Even if the rest of the meal is mediocre, the smell of freshly baking bread will make everything else taste good. We had an ample supply of the old bread that the grocery stores wanted to get rid of, so we were eating that. Sometimes we would put a little butter on one side and run it through the oven so that it didn't taste like it was a week old, but it sure didn't taste fresh either.

I surveyed what equipment we had available. There were no muffin pans in the kitchen. Muffins are easy, but you have to have pans. A trip to the restaurant supply store, $100 spent, and we had enough pans to bake everyone a fresh muffin. I try to lead by suggestion and example, but I wanted no uncertainty as to where we needed to go with food quality. I issued the order that freshly baked bread of some sort would be served at least every other day. I brought in some recipes, and my orders were reluctantly followed.

I had printed up about ten copies of the new rules and posted one copy on the door leading into the dining room and another copy on the wall at the beginning of the serving line. I wanted to give everyone about two weeks' notice of the changes. I had printed extra copies because I expected to replace a few after residents expressed their feelings by writing editorials on the notices. To my surprise, no disparaging remarks were ever written on the papers. Someone did highlight the changes by underlining key provisions and placing stars in the margins.

Meals started getting significantly better in the two weeks prior to the Monday start date. Some friends from supporting churches came into the Mission in the afternoons to prepare their favorite economical meal with our chefs so that our staff could learn more meal variety. The muffin pans were getting used, and we slowly moved from basic corn to blueberry and then apple-cinnamon.

Other than providing a few suggestions of a meal based on what was on sale at the grocery store, I never had to issue any more orders about food quality. As the food improved, the people would go out of their way to congratulate the chefs on their fine work. That little bit of thanks got the creativity rolling and, within a week, the quality of the food was exceeding my expectations.

Finally, the Monday for food sales arrived. I had met with the staff to iron out as many details as we could foresee. Most of the concerns of the staff and the Board were how to handle the money. We drew up a weekly sign up sheet for staff members to man the payment table and use the metal cash box I ordered from eBay for $15, including shipping. I put my name on the list for cash box duties Monday for both lunch and dinner. I didn't know what to expect from our guests, and, if there was a riot, I needed to be the one to take the heat.

Lunch went very smoothly, but the crowd was smaller than usual.

The chefs wanted to hit it big for dinner. The menu was posted by 2:00 p.m. Roasted lemon-pepper chicken, light or dark meat quarters—your choice. In the past, most of the chicken meat had been shredded into a casserole or soup to make it stretch. An entire chicken quarter for yourself—that was big.

The rules had now been posted for two weeks, so almost everyone knew what to expect. But the quality of the meal was beyond their expectations. I had allowed some spies into the kitchen about an hour before meal service as taste-testers to be sure the chicken was good enough to serve to all of our guests. Each of them was given a few bites which they savored thoroughly. I listened to their praises and then watched as they went outside and began spreading the word concerning what awaited our evening guests.

I sat down at the table in front of the entrance to the dining room with the cash box in front of me and anxiously gave the nod to the chef to announce that dinner was served and to unlock the door. The very first man through the door messed up my carefully planned system when he pulled out his wallet and produced a twenty-dollar bill. I had enough change in the box to handle a ten, but I could not change a twenty.

"I should have change in a few minutes. Please sit down and enjoy your meal and I will bring you your change."

He had no problem with the arrangement and the look on his face was one of satisfaction that he had been able to produce a twenty-dollar bill. Observing my frustration, he remarked rather proudly, "Sorry, I don't have anything smaller."

After about two dozen people had filed by my table, a man in a wheelchair rolled himself into the dining room. But, seeing me collecting cash, he started to turn his chair around to leave.

"Excuse me, sir. Please come in. There is no charge for your meal. Please sit over here." I grabbed the handles on the back of his chair and wheeled him to the table next to mine. I wasn't going to charge a person in a wheelchair.

"Let me get a plate for you. We are having lemon-pepper chicken this evening. Would you like white or dark meat?"

"Dark, please."

I brought his plate and then resumed my position at the cash table. I glanced over every few minutes to watch him taking big bites of chicken and then sucking on the bones.

When he had cleaned his plate, I watched him lean back in his chair and reach down for something in his pocket. He turned his chair around and rolled toward me. Then he reached out his hand and handed me six quarters.

"Thank you, that was mighty good."

Everything was going surprisingly smoothly until a young man appearing in his late 20s with disheveled blonde hair walked through the door. He stared at me sitting at the first table with the cash box in front of me.

"What's this!"

"Dinner is a dollar fifty this evening. Will you be joining us?"

He then launched into a string of vulgarity in his attempt to express his displeasure with our food charging policy, the quality of our food, and the services which he thought we should be giving to him.

One of our larger resident guests got up and offered to escort this man outside. Since his conversation was becoming more vulgar and there were many children in the dining room, I agreed that it was time for him to go.

His parting words were, "I'm calling my lawyer!"

I never heard from his lawyer, but I did mull over his words for many weeks to come.

If my actions over the last fifteen years had contributed to producing this sort of entitlement mentality, God forgive me for my ignorance.

On Wednesday morning I came into the Mission early to start another special meal. I was determined that if people were going to be paying for our meals, they certainly were going to get loads of value for their money.

I started the fire in our new, one-ton, iron smoker and was preparing to place ten whole turkeys in the smoking chamber. I had mixed up a concoction of olive oil, Cajun seasonings, and cayenne pepper and injected about two tablespoons of the solution into each side of each turkey breast. Then I rubbed the left-over solution over the skin of all the turkeys. My plan was to let the temperature in the smoking chamber get no higher than 180 degrees so that no moisture was boiled out of the meat and let them smoke for about ten hours.

We had purchased our smoker from a man in central Texas who welded them to the customers' specifications. Ours was a special order that came to $3900, but one of our donors who believed in the value of our food upgrades paid the entire bill. The smoker had been with us for only one month and still attracted lots of attention when smoke started rising from the chimneys.

As I was stoking the fire, a young man came up to me.

"What are you fixin' to cook?"

"We are having smoked turkey for dinner."

"You know, Mr. Blake, I sure appreciate the changes you have made. These chores you require of us, that ain't nothing that we shouldn't have been doing anyway, and the food sure has gotten a whole lot better."

About twenty minutes later a man walked up to me who was about 6'3", 220 pounds, and appeared to be in very healthy condition.

"What you doing?"

"We are serving smoked turkey for dinner. Would you like a peek?"

I lifted the lid to reveal a row of turkeys under a layer of mesquite wood smoke.

"Will you be joining us for dinner?"

"Hmmm. I think I better go get a job."

He was back at 5:00 p.m. with his $1.50 in hand.

Another individual who stood out in my memory in the first week of food charging was a man whom I knew had been living in the homeless camp behind the Mission. He would come in and pay for his meal; get up and leave, and then a few minutes later return to the entrance line with one of his friends. When they approached the cash box table, he would pull out his wallet and hand over the money so that his friend could eat. He knew better than to give his friend the money before they had made it through the line to the cash box.

Within a month, however, the homeless camp had disbanded. For the fifteen years that I had been directing the Mission, there had always been a camp which varied between 10-30 people who lived by the railroad tracks behind the Mission. They preferred to camp out rather than to sleep on our property because they did not want to comply with our rules of no alcohol or illegal drugs. These people obviously had money from some source because they were always drinking, and I knew the Circle K was not giving the beer away. Our new policies now forced them to allocate their financial resources between food and beer. All of them chose beer.

About three years earlier I had an encounter which broke my heart. I met a young lady downtown who had an infant with her. She was obviously homeless. I started talking with her but didn't tell her who I was. After a few minutes I suggested, "You should go to the Rescue Mission. Do you know where it is?"

"Oh no, I went there a month ago, but some of the men they had hanging around that place scared me, and I didn't feel safe."

The statement pierced my chest like a dagger. I knew that she was talking about some of the drunks from the homeless camp who would come in for a meal in the evenings.

I was haunted by her statement for years, not knowing how to change the situation to make it more inviting for her. I wanted to have an open invitation to the people from the camps to come in and experience the possibility of change for a better life. Yet my experience was that far less than 1% ever took me up on the offer. But within a month of charging for food, the homeless camp was gone, and all of the problem people left without my ever having to confront the situation directly.

I learned that no one shelter can serve all of the people all of the time. If we are to keep our doors open to the obnoxious drunks from the camp, then we were not going to be able to serve this woman and her child who would prefer to sleep in a back alley than to be around the drunks from the camp. Since I have to choose, I would rather serve the woman and her child.

CHAPTER 20

MARCELA & CASSANDRA

MARCELA CAME INTO MY OFFICE holding some papers which were stapled together. The process server had just delivered a divorce petition to her. Some of the other women in the Mission told her I was a lawyer.

I invited her to sit down and fill me in on the details. Her face held the expression of complete panic. She had been living near San Diego with her husband and Cassandra, their seven year-old daughter. Life got rough after he lost his job. He came to El Paso to visit his parents. After a couple of months he sent her money to send Cassandra to El Paso. She reluctantly agreed to send her. Once Cassandra was in El Paso, however, he told her that he was not returning to California and that Cassandra was not returning either.

She was left without rent money and without her daughter. She sold everything she could to buy a bus ticket and came to El Paso to find Cassandra, but once she got to El Paso her husband's family refused to let her see her daughter. Now they had hired a lawyer to file for divorce, and she was in fear that she would never see her daughter again.

The months of stress had taken its toll. She took almost an hour to tell me these few details as she would start crying hysterically and had to take time out to compose herself. For most of the hour, she was shaking as she spoke.

On one of her breaks to wipe away tears and wash her face, I was able to read through the entire divorce petition. When she came back into my office, I started talking to give her a little break.

"The good news here is that I am confident that the court will order a visitation schedule so that you will be able to see Cassandra pretty soon. Now, let's talk about the legal procedures going forward. The first thing that you need to know is that the judge doesn't care about you. In a divorce case involving a child, the only person the judge cares about is the child. The legal standard for everything is, 'What is in the best interest of the child?' Your husband has a house. It is not his house, but he still has a house. You are living in a homeless shelter. I think it is a very nice shelter, but the judge has never been here for a visit. All he knows is that it is a homeless shelter. The judge is not going to order Cassandra to come live in a shelter. In order for you to receive a favorable custody order, you will need to prove to the judge that you have the ability to care for Cassandra other than just by receiving child support. That means that before this case gets in front of the judge, you need to have a job and rent an apartment."

We covered a few more issues, and I asked her some questions to make sure that she had heard me correctly. My advice seemed to make her feel a little better. She actually started to smile a bit when I told her that I would represent her as she was afraid of being out-gunned by going to court without a lawyer. Once she had left, I typed up an answer and called the opposing lawyer to see if a friendly child visitation schedule could be arranged. Our opponent was fairly certain that his client would not agree to any visitation. The divorce petition came with a court setting for temporary orders, but it was three weeks away.

That afternoon I drove to the courthouse to file the answer and stopped by our court to obtain an earlier hearing date so that Marcela would not have to wait the three weeks to see her daughter. The new court settings came with a final hearing date in mid-December which was five months away. I returned to the Mission to advise Marcela how much time she had to get her life in order.

As I expected, we came away from the temporary orders hearing with a child visitation order, but it was much more of a fight than I had anticipated. The husband's lawyer raised allegations of Marcela's emotional instability and of her being a flight risk by possibly taking Cassandra into Mexico where she would be beyond the jurisdictional reach of the El Paso court. The judge's decision was that the husband was to deliver Cassandra to the Rescue Mission each Saturday morning and then pick her up at 3:00 p.m. that same day. Marcela had only 6 hours of visitation time per week. Furthermore, she was prohibited from leaving the grounds of the Mission with Cassandra, and the judge placed the additional burden on me of designating someone to watch Marcela to ensure that she did not leave the Mission's grounds.

It was one of the most restrictive child visitation orders that I had ever received. I was not pleased. Marcela, on the other hand, thought some visitation was better than none and left the court knowing that she would soon be able to see her daughter for the first time in four months. I was on notice that the judge had already taken the other side of this case and that we had an uphill battle to make Marcela the custodial parent.

I sat down with Marcela again the next week, after her first child visitation session, and expressed my concerns that we were already out of favor with the judge and that she really needed to get moving if she was to win the custody fight. To her credit, it didn't take much to light a fire under her. Within a week she had a job as a waitress at the Hacienda Restaurant across the street from the Mission. I was happy to buy her the two blouses that she would need as her waitress uniforms. I am always pleased to invest in the economic progress of our guests.

I didn't hear much from Marcela over the next couple of months. Child visitation continued with no unusual events each Saturday, and Marcela scheduled her working hours so that she always had Saturdays off. Since I worked at the Mission on most Saturdays, I was able to meet Cassandra and watch the two interact in the dining room and at the Mission's playground. The only issue that I observed about Marcela's ability to be a good mother was her propensity to pile all sorts of desserts on Cassandra's tray, even though Cassandra would have been better served by a fitness program. As lawyer-client relations go, she did the work she needed to do and left me in blissful quiet—particularly so considering that she was living only thirty yards from her lawyer's office.

Around the middle of November I received a phone call from a man who told me he was managing some apartments about a mile up the hill from the Mission. He said that a lady from the Mission had rented an apartment from him starting at the first of the month but that she had never moved in.

"If she is not going to live here, then let me rent it to someone else. She paid cash for the deposit and all of the November rent. I never had anyone rent an apartment and not move in. I just don't understand what is going on?"

"Hmm. I think I know who that might be. Let me have your number, and I will call you back."

That afternoon when Marcela returned from the lunch shift at the Hacienda, I called her into my office.

"Marcela, did you go rent an apartment?"

"Yes."

"Then why are you still here?"

"You told me I had to rent an apartment before December. You didn't tell me I have to go live in it."

I didn't quite know what to say. But I was getting a little insight into what it must have been like to live with Marcela.

I reiterated that the purpose for the apartment was to show that she had the capacity to care for Cassandra *away* from the Mission. "Yes, you have to move into it."

After another week, however, Marcela still had not budged from her room at the Mission. Then I started getting other reports from our counselors. At first Marcela was in a room with two other roommates. It was about twelve feet square with one bunk bed, a single bed, and a window. The community bath was down the hall. But Marcela had been gathering so much clothing and other stuff that had been donated to the Mission that the other women moved out because there was no more space for them.

The next time I saw Marcela, I reminded her that she needed to move into her own space and that I was willing to provide the Mission's truck and trailer to assist with moving her things.

Another week went by.

Finally, we had to change the message.

"Marcela, this shelter is for people who are homeless. You have your own place to live. You need to leave so that other women who need this space are able to move in. If you are not out by three o'clock Friday afternoon, we will put your things in plastic bags and store them for you, but you will not be staying here after three o'clock on Friday. Do you understand?"

The Friday deadline gave her another four days to pack and move.

Nothing happened.

On Friday morning I walked back to Marcela's room to inspect the progress. Marcela was not there. I had heard stories from the counselors about the room, but I did not imagine how bad it really was. Every bed had piles of things on them. All floor space was covered, too, except for a path about six inches wide between the door and her bed.

I returned for another inspection around one o'clock. Nothing done.

Now it was time to mobilize the troops. I notified two of my counselors of our afternoon task and took an inventory of plastic trash bags.

At three I gathered the two counselors and we marched toward the women's rooms. Marcela was no where to be found, and nothing had been done in her room. I reluctantly peeled three plastic bags off of the roll, and we started to work. The first task was to shove enough stuff away from the door so that the three of us could stand in the room at the same time. Then we began stuffing our bags. Once a bag was filled, we tied it at the top and placed it in the hall.

After an hour, I took a break from bagging to back the truck and trailer next to the exit door because the hall was already congested to the point that no one could pass.

About 4:30 Marcela showed up. After a few minutes of screaming at us for doing what we had told her we were going to do, she consented to help out in the bagging process. One of the objects that could not go in a bag was a television with a 19-inch screen. It was sitting on the floor in the hall waiting for its spot in the trailer. Marcela had found a large black Magic Marker and was making sure that all of her things were clearly labeled. I watched her walk up to the television set and write "MARCELA" in big, black, permanent ink right across the front of the screen.

All of her things were finally loaded a little after five o'clock, and we started the task of sweeping and mopping the space for the next guest.

The Rescue Mission trailer is actually a 16-foot long Trails West horse trailer which I had special ordered without the horse dividers. It is 7 feet, four inches wide and 7 feet tall. Marcela's sacks filled almost two-thirds of it all the way to the ceiling.

I didn't see Marcela again until the next Wednesday when she came to ask me if I would pull the trailer up the hill to her apartment.

The court sent us notice in the first week of December that our case would not be reached for trial, and we were reset for April. Marcela had more time to get her act together; however, at this point I was dreading how she would do on the witness stand, and I knew that additional time wouldn't really help.

Meanwhile, I could report to the court that my client had succeeded in being gainfully employed for over three months, had managed to gather a variety of home furnishings, and had procured her own accommodations. The judge lifted the restriction on child visitation occurring only at the Mission, and Marcela was free to meet with Cassandra at her own home or wherever else she would like to go.

Court day was not fun. Most cases come down to a somewhat civilized version of a back alley fight with people in pressed suits using polished words to kill their opponent's case using any means possible within the rules—or some bent version thereof. Only it is not a case of whoever hired the best tongue wins. The lawyer has to have something truthful and positive to say. I really hate losing, even when I know going in that I don't have a chance.

The judge's ruling was answered with Marcela's screaming and wailing in such a manner that the bailiff had to escort her out of the court.

I did not see or hear from Marcela for over a year after the court date. She did not even come pick up a copy of the court's order after it had been printed up and signed by the judge.

A year and a half later, Marcela and Cassandra came to the Mission's dining room on Thanksgiving Day. I was surprised to see them because I knew that the court's restrictive order did not call for Thanksgiving visitation. I walked over to greet them and see how things were going.

Less than a year from the judge's ruling, Marcela's husband had found a new girlfriend who didn't want Cassandra hanging around. He called up Marcela and told her to take Cassandra back.

As I was listening to Marcela's story, I kept glancing at Cassandra's face. She kept eating her Thanksgiving lunch, said nothing, and showed no emotion at all. She was now nine years old. I cannot imagine the pain of being stolen from your mother, dragged through a court custody fight, and then told by the winning party that you weren't really wanted after all. I guess she had been cut so deeply that she couldn't bleed any more.

CHAPTER 21

MR. LOPEZ' ARMOIRE

MR. LOPEZ WAS STANDING ON the front porch of the Mission leaning against the rail and watching traffic go by. He stopped me as I was leaving.

"Are you the Director?"

"Yes."

"Hospice told me to come over here and stay here until I died. I have worked all of my life. I can't just sit here and do nothing. Don't you have any work that I can do?"

Mr. Lopez was about 60 years old and appeared to have some type of liver condition. His skin and the whites of his eyes were yellowed. His abdomen was bloated, but he was not fat. His hands belonged to a working man. They had a texture developed from years of gripping hammers and shovels.

Whatever I had been leaving the office to do was no longer important. He was not asking for money but for the privilege of doing productive work. I had a great sense of respect for his work ethic. He seemed to be at peace with his medical issues. He was not looking for my sympathy, but he caught it anyway.

"Yes, I do have a job! Do you know about our furniture shop?"

Rescue Industries had been open about a year. Our first product was the pine bunk bed that we were using in our own dormitories. We were doing a pretty good job in the manufacturing process. Our start was from the combined experiences of our first few homeless employees and my two years of wood shop in 8th and 9th grade. As we hired more homeless workers, each one would bring knowledge of a different tool or technique, and our combined skill level gradually rose, while the quality of our products continually improved.

I asked Mr. Lopez if he had any carpentry experience as the two of us walked toward the shop. He did not profess an expertise in carpentry, but I had the impression that he had done a little of everything and probably possessed a knowledge of woodworking that was considerably more advanced than ours was at that time.

The wood shop was a good 300 yards from the front door of the Mission, and Mr. Lopez had no problem keeping up with me as we walked and talked.

When we got to the shop, I started showing him around and introducing him to other workers. He was very interested in the collection of planers, saws, sanders, and drill presses that we had accumulated. At one end of the shop, our workers were putting the last few bolts into a completed bunk bed. Mr. Lopez was very complimentary of the design and said how much he had enjoyed sleeping on one in the dorm.

"When the guy on the top comes down the ladder, the rest of the bed does not shake!"

"Yes, I made sure of that. When we first designed this bed, we set one up in the chapel for an experiment. I found one of our Mission residents who was over 250 pounds and told him I would pay him $20 if he could break it. He climbed onto the upper bunk, jumped up and down and shook it from every direction. He couldn't break it, but I saw some of the joints between the bed box and the corner posts moving a bit, so we designed these corner braces. Now it doesn't move at all. Since we have the bed construction down, we need to design an armoire which will fit at the end of the bunk bed. Do you think you could help us with that one?"

Mr. Lopez was excited about the challenge of starting on a new project from scratch. I showed him where the time cards were to clock in, and we had a new employee.

He spent his first few days helping with bunk bed assembly so that he could learn what we were doing and whom he was working with. When everyone else took a break, Mr. Lopez would draw up designs for the armoire so that he could present me with a materials list. Within a week he came to see me with his drawings. He had designed an armoire that would fit between the corner posts at the end of a bunk bed. It had two doors that opened from the center and drawers on the bottom. Most of the materials were already in the shop, but he did leave me with a short shopping list for additional materials.

All of the supplies were in by the next week, and Mr. Lopez dove into the armoire project. Each day that I walked through the shop, Mr. Lopez would greet me enthusiastically and tell me about all of the progress he had made. His energy level was actually rising as the armoire was coming together.

Once the frame had been completed and the side panels were installed, his mind raced ahead to other products that we could build and market with the equipment we had.

The completed armoire was truly a thing of beauty. He had spent days sanding it and then staining it with a golden oak finish and adding a protective coat of polyurethane. His face beamed with pride as he showed me his finished work, and I couldn't help noticing how his abdomen seemed less bloated and his eyes had a sparkle that was not there before. Then he started telling me his ideas for design changes on the next models so that construction would be more efficient and we could start producing several of them at a time.

His excitement for life seemed to grow by the day, so I was shocked to walk toward the shop about 9:00 a.m. one morning and find Mr. Lopez sitting by himself with his head in his hands. He looked like he had been crying. When he saw me, he jumped up.

"Mr. Barrow, I need to talk to you. The hospice nurse came to see me this morning. She told me that I am now too healthy to receive services from them any more. If I am no longer on hospice care, can I still work here at the Mission?"

"Sure you can."

I gave him a hug, and the smile returned to his face.

But in another three weeks he had a medical relapse and went to the hospital where he stayed for about a week. The hospital discharged him to a nursing facility as he was no longer able to care for himself. He died about two weeks later.

I never could sell Mr. Lopez' armoire. We kept it for our own use. I fondly remember the pride and enthusiasm that he had in working with his hands and teaching others in our shop how to make better products. Most of all, I remember Mr. Lopez for the lessons that he taught me of the pleasure of helping people receiving hospice care. What a joy and a privilege to be able to share the love of Jesus with those who are in their last days!

CHAPTER 22

FAILURE JUST JUMPS
UP AND BITES ME

MICHAEL WAS A HOMELESS MAN who was staying at the
Rescue Mission. I had hired him to work in the furniture shop, and
he had been there for about four weeks.

I have learned to take Sundays off. When I first started at the
Mission, I would work every day because there were still more
problems that I had not yet solved. After about three years, I learned
that I can work nonstop and still not solve all of the problems, but,
in the process, I will lose my health and my family.

On this particular weekend, our furniture crew had been
working on Saturday to try to catch up with a big order that needed
to be shipped last week. We were making bunk beds and chests of
drawers to be trucked to California to a fellow mission.

I came to the shop after church and lunch on Sunday to see

the progress that had been made the previous day. On my way out I passed the time clock and the board we had made with slots to hold all of the time cards. Saturday work was optional for our crew unless we were really behind and I had to call an "all hands on deck" emergency. I wanted to see who had been working and for how long.

The time clock had a slot at its base with an arrow pointing to the spot where the clock would print the time on the card. Most of the workers had clocked in by 7:30 on Saturday morning, and almost all of them had left by noon. Of the ten workers we had that Saturday, one had clocked out at 11:30 a.m., and all the rest clocked out between 11:58 and 12:00.

Except for Michael.

Interestingly, his card did not have the printed number from the time clock, but, instead, he had hand-written 3:00 p.m. on the card as his exit time. I removed his card from the file and stuck it into my pocket as I wanted to ask him about it before the card got processed with the rest of payroll on Monday.

I walked to the kitchen to see how lunch service had gone. When I approached the front desk, I was surprised to see Michael sitting near the desk.

"Hey, how is it going?"

"Good."

"I saw you put in a pretty long day yesterday. Did you get some good work done?"

"Yes sir, I did."

"What time did you finally quit?"

"Three o'clock."

"Really, who were you working with?

"Matthew."

"The whole day?"

"Yes sir."

"I don't think so. Matthew clocked out at noon."

Michael just stared blankly at me.

"You're fired."

By the time I got to work on Monday our counselors already knew the story and were asking me if I wanted Michael out of the Mission.

"No, we don't need to evict him, but he will not work for us any more."

Two days later I had to retract those words. Once the story got around that Michael had falsified his time card and was trying to steal from the Mission, other Mission residents were so enraged that I was concerned for his safety. The shop was financially fragile, and our workers knew it might be in danger of closing if the red ink got too heavy. The thought of one of their fellow workers contributing to the red ink by stealing, after the Mission had provided him a job, made their blood boil. I had to tell Michael that for his own safety, he needed to leave.

Michael met with Diego, one of our counselors, for advice as to where he should go after leaving the Mission. Michael told Diego that he was not really surprised that things had gone this way. He looked Diego straight in the eye and said, "Every time things get going really well for me, failure just jumps up and bites me."

Amazingly, he had no sense of personal responsibility for losing his job or for being asked to leave the Mission. He talked about it as if "failure" was some overpowering outside force that just had it in for him, and he was doomed from the start.

I heard about Michael again almost eight years later. He was still homeless and was staying in another shelter primarily funded with government money where no beds were provided and all of the residents slept on the floor.

Back to the parable of the sower and the seeds: I can teach. I can lead. I can set an example. I can encourage. I can make opportunities available. I can even invest in the clothing, materials, and equipment a person may need to do a job. But I cannot force people to take responsibility for their own actions. So, some eight years later, after having availed himself of all of the rehabilitative services that several shelters had to provide, Michael is still homeless—go figure?

We may create programs to provide housing, and we may feed those who are homeless, but a sandwich never saved a soul. Perhaps the sandwich can draw a person to a place where he or she can hear the Gospel. But Michael had to decide for himself that he wanted the change that Jesus provides.

CHAPTER 23

TRUCK-BED

I WAS PRAYING ABOUT A way to show off how strong our bunk beds are. Then God gave me an idea. We had just bought a new forklift for the shop. I could pick up a car with the forklift, put it on top of the bunk bed, and take pictures of it for an advertising flier to distribute to potential customers. My next thought was that a VW Beetle would not do. I needed something that looked really big and heavy. I needed a Chevy Suburban.

The only problem was that I did not know anyone who owned a Suburban. I did have a good friend who had just bought a brand new F-150. I thought that might work pretty well, so I gave him a call. At first he was willing to loan me his truck, but when he found out what I was going to do with it, he retracted his offer. So I prayed, "Lord, this is a great plan, but I need you to provide the Suburban."

Meanwhile, I went out to the shop and told some of our workers what I had in mind. I wanted a twin over full bunk bed in the extra-long size, so that it would have a larger and more stable foot-print than the standard twin over twin. All of the joints had to be absolutely perfect as we were going to put a Suburban on it. "By the way, I think the Golden Oak finish will look very nice in the pictures."

Some of the workers in the shop were scratching their heads and looking at me like I had lost a few screws, but they started building the bed.

A couple of days later one of our volunteers who had been a building contractor came to the Mission to see me. He brought his engineering books and his calculator.

"Blake, I heard about what you are planning and it isn't going to work."

He proceeded to show me the load-bearing calculations for the four-by-four corner posts for the bunk bed from his engineering book. Then he calculated that we had weakened each post by a factor of 50% due to the notches that we cut out for the two bed boxes. His calculations were that the bed would crumble with 3500 pounds on it, and the Suburban weighed about 6000.

"The numbers aren't even close, you are going to kill somebody. Don't do it."

I had respect for all of his educated calculations, so I began to doubt that I had really heard the voice of the Lord. Since my first year at the Mission, I would make my decisions through prayer and listening to the voice of God. Basically, I just prayed and listened, and then did what I felt God was telling me to do. God's voice seemed so clear to me about the Suburban. How could I have been wrong?

I spent the next couple of days in a state of directionless depression over my apparent inability to hear God clearly. I continued to pray and tried to listen.

Then the call came from the front desk clerk. "There is a man up here who wants to donate a Chevy Suburban to the Mission. He says it still runs, but it sure is ugly. We don't want that, do we?"

"YES, YES!" I was practically yelling through the phone. "Tell him to stay right there; I will be right up to the front."

I hung up the phone and almost ran to the front desk. The man looked a little puzzled as I enthusiastically shook his hand and thanked him profusely for the generous donation of this priceless old vehicle.

He began to explain as we stepped out toward the front driveway, "It doesn't get very good gas mileage, and the paint is pretty worn. Twenty years in the El Paso sun will do that."

"It is absolutely beautiful!" I interrupted as I gazed upon his faded purple Suburban. I assured him that I had the perfect place for it.

I had been working at the Mission for seven years at that time. We never had a Suburban, or anything else near that size, donated to us, and we have never had another one since then.

I had heard the voice of God after all! I prayed for a Suburban and, in less than a week, here it is.

After he signed over the title, I ran to the shop to tell our crew to hurry up with the finish.

We set the bunk bed up in the parking lot on the side of the Mission, but our little Toyota forklift wouldn't budge against the Suburban. No problem. I went to see our friends at McKinney Wrecking behind the Mission and asked to borrow their 10,000-pound forklift. Fortunately, they didn't ask me what we needed it for. They just handed me the key.

We had a camera set up on a tripod to catch the whole show. Just in case anyone might have thought that we pulled the engine out to lighten the load, we drove the Suburban up to the bunk bed and parked it parallel to the bed. The driver got out, waved to the camera, and stepped into the giant forklift. Both forks went under the Suburban, and he hoisted it into the air. I was on the other side of the bunk bed guiding our forklift driver on the proper height and placement of the Suburban. We moved the Suburban over the top of the bunk bed and then gently set it down on the four corner posts. The wood did not even creak or crackle when the forks dropped below the undercarriage and then backed away.

What a beautiful sight! There was our super-strong bunk bed holding up under the weight of a Chevy Suburban in spite of all of the engineering calculations. We took a dozen pictures from all angles and then brought the forklift back to remove the Suburban.

I prepared the best picture into an advertising flier, and we compiled a mailing list of over 500 missions and summer camps. Anyone who housed a lot of people and needed indestructible bunk beds would want our products.

I gathered a few of our homeless residents to assist with the folding of the fliers and stuffing them into the envelopes. One of the men stuffing envelopes looked at the picture and then at me.

"What's the matter," he asked, "were you afraid to sit on the bed?"

After all of the prayer, effort, and sweat that I had gone through in getting the pictures while keeping everyone well away from the bed just in case it did suddenly give way, I was furious at his comment.

It took me another day to calm down and realize that I was wrong and this man was right. He may have been the only one rude enough to have made such a comment, but if he was thinking that, then others would be thinking it also. I didn't do the picture correctly.

We got the camera set up again, and I went to borrow the forklift. The second filming went just as smoothly as the first. Again, the bed didn't make a sound when the full weight of the Suburban dropped down on it.

Now I was on. I had to go sit on the bed for the picture.

Unfortunately, we discovered that my face was in the shadow of the truck when I sat on the bed, so we took a few more pictures with me under the engine as if I were trying to change its oil.

That picture would work just fine. We tore up all of the old fliers and made new ones with the new picture.

Interestingly, the bed we built for the photo shoot became an instant sales hit. The next day a man offered me $1000 for it —considerably above our published sales price. The next week another man offered us top dollar for the Suburban even though the forklift had cut a nasty scratch into the side door. The buyer said the scratch made it even more valuable as others would know it was caused by the forklift. He insisted on several pictures to go with the purchase.

Over the years that picture has helped make sales of well over a thousand bunk beds while making more jobs available for people who are homeless at the Mission.

CHAPTER 24

NINE WAYS A MISSION-RUN BUSINESS HELPS THE RECOVERING ADDICT

I RECEIVED A PHONE CALL from the person at the Association of Gospel Rescue Missions who was putting all of the details together for the next annual convention in six weeks in Chicago. He had an opening for a seminar speaker.

"We want you to teach a seminar called 'Nine Ways a Mission-Run Business Helps the Recovering Addict.'"

"OK, apparently you already have nine ideas in mind."

"No, that just sounded like a good number. You can change it into whatever number you want to."

I had taught seminars during the previous two annual conventions on creating a social enterprise within a mission, so I knew the format. Each seminar was 75 minutes long. While my previous seminars were very well received, I had already presented that information twice. If I agreed to teach another one, I was determined that all of the information would be new.

This topic was an intriguing new slant on the subject. My last seminar was how to create the social enterprise, and what that social enterprise could do for a mission. This topic was from the opposite perspective—what the social enterprise could do for the homeless guests of our missions. Somehow I allowed my excitement for the subject matter to take control of my speech, and I heard myself saying, "OK, I will do it."

I hung up the phone and pulled out a blank legal pad. I wrote the number "one" in the left margin followed by "self-esteem." Then I wrote the number "two" on the next line and stared at the paper trying to think of what else to write. All I could think of was building self-esteem. While certainly important, I wasn't going to talk for 75 minutes just on self-esteem, and no one would want to hear it either.

After about ten minutes of staring at the page, Jimmy walked into my office to let me know they needed more supplies in the shop. He saw me staring at the paper and asked what was up.

"The people at AGRM want me to teach a seminar on all the ways that a mission-run business helps the recovering addict, but all I can think of is that getting a job builds self-esteem. I need to think up at least nine ways. I have to talk for 75 minutes on it, and I don't know what else to say."

"Hmm. Let me think on that. Meanwhile, we need another thousand board feet of red oak to finish the last order."

The next morning Jimmy was back in my office. "Hey Boss, did you think of any more ways?"

"No, my brain is still stuck on self-esteem."

"Well, we've got you covered. I asked around the shop and everyone has ideas. But we have way more than nine."

Of course! Why didn't it occur to me to go ask the people we were helping how they thought they were being helped?

I scheduled a staff lunch for all of our furniture workers on Friday. We ordered enough pizzas and sodas for everyone to have plenty, and we sat around a large conference table so my workers could educate me on the benefits of the system I had created for them.

I thanked everyone for the ideas they had reported to Jimmy and suggested that we go around the room and let each person say how working in a business run by the Mission was helping them in their recoveries from drug or alcohol addictions. I turned the pages of my legal pad back to my writing of self-esteem and nothing more, and I got ready to take notes as fast as I could.

Jimmy was sitting closest to me, and he was the first to start.

"I never want to forget where I came from. We are the witnesses of what God can do—the people society has thrown away and God has rebuilt. When another recovering addict comes into the shop who has less clean time than I do, I see myself in that person, and I remember where I have been. Recovery from an addiction is a gift from God. We can't hoard that gift. We have to share it with others. We are all important to God."

Nelson was next: "Working here brought me to understand how I got to this point in my life. It was through isolation. Whenever I had a problem, I would run away by myself. But everyplace I ran, the problems were still there. They followed me. God opened my eyes here and brought me to the point of realizing that I needed to surrender everything to God. I couldn't isolate here. You forced me to work with others in a team. Then I began to see how others, who had the same problems as I did, had realized tremendous potential. God told me I had potential, too, although I never believed it before. As I started thinking that maybe I did have potential, I discovered it was true. Now I am amazed by the things I help make with my hands. I never knew I had value before."

Melissa was the next to speak: "The most important thing is praying together at the beginning and end of each shift. Prayer brought us together into one family. We can relate to each other's problems because we all come from our addictions. We go to God together, and then we help each other through each problem."

Robert said, "Work is my support group. All of us are trying to stay clean in a setting where Jesus is. I look around me, and I see others who have been through the same problems that I have, and they are still clean. Then I know that I can do it, too."

David said, "This job forced me to learn patience and compassion."

Bruce's comments brought lots of nods of agreement: "I fell down and got drunk. You came to find me when I was still sauced. I awoke in my drunkenness and saw you standing over me. You told me that I was needed and I was important. Nobody ever told me that before. When I came back to work, everyone welcomed me. They didn't criticize me for falling down. Praying became part of the job. We listen to K-Love all day. The music keeps me focused on our purpose, which is to serve God. I learned I wasn't strong enough spiritually to overcome the temptations. But this environment of K-Love and constant prayer now has me growing spiritually."

James said that he had learned respect for others and learned how to work with others. "You have to; Jesus is here."

Mick immediately jumped in to echo James' response: "I feel the presence of God in that building. God has to be there or we wouldn't get out such great products, because we are just a bunch of screw-ups."

John's comment was on a more earthly level: "It occupies my time and keeps my mind focused on building things instead of negative things. If I don't stay busy, I am going to end up drinking."

Felton said, "I thought I was trash when I became homeless, but all these homeless people I work with—they are just like everyone else."

Ramon said, "I have a future now. When I was struggling with addiction, I lost everything. I have my self-esteem back; I have my family back, and now I have even more family. I have my Mission family. The Mission has always been there for me when I needed help."

Finally, someone mentioned self-esteem.

Michael said, "I was a true loner. I didn't like being with people. I guess that is because I had never met other people who accepted me. Now I like being here with these folks, and I find great satisfaction in helping others."

When Carmen spoke, I had to write fast to get every word. It helped that she was speaking slowly while tears were rolling down her face. "I came to the Mission almost five years ago on June 13, 2004. I had no intention of getting better. I had given up. I went through the Relapse Prevention Program, and I invited Jesus into my life. It is only through him that all this is possible. Jesus went to those who had the least, and he saw them with compassion. This is ministry. It is not like a regular job. I care about other people now, and I want to be there for them. The Mission doesn't give up on us. We show compassion without judgment. In any other place we would keep it a secret that we are addicts. God has healed me now, so I can help heal others."

Jill said, "I don't have any family support—none at all. They are convinced that I am a waste of space. These people here are now my family. It doesn't matter how horrible my day is. I know that someone here is going to make me smile, and that's huge."

William jumped in, "When I started to relapse, others here saw it in me before I could feel it myself. They took me aside and prayed with me. Then we talked through some issues that were pushing me back to the bottle. We went to God together asking God for help. They reminded me that whenever I felt the urge to drink, I should stop and read the Bible instead. One week I spent almost every waking hour outside of work reading scripture. Then I discovered that the more scripture I read, the more strength I had to turn away from that bottle."

Chris was next, "I hated myself. I knew I was worthless because my parents told me so. I needed the drugs to cover up the way I saw myself. But when I came to work here, I met other addicts who were just like me, and together we made beautiful things that people would pay their money for. Then we gained an appreciation for each other, because none of us could make these things by ourselves. I learned that I had talents. I had not known that. As we prayed together and looked to each other for support, that appreciation grew into stronger bonds of love than I have ever had with any of my own family members. The only reason that I am still clean today is because of this new family that I have sitting in this room."

Ken described watching a customer coming into the shop. The customer stopped over a chest of drawers that he had helped finish. "I watched him as he kept rubbing his hands over the finish and saying how smooth the finish was. Then he pulled out his checkbook and wrote a check for the price of the chest, and we loaded it into his pickup truck. I just stood amazed that this man had paid his money for the work I had done."

In such a large group, there are always some who sit at the back and won't speak up. Carolyn had been sitting in the corner, back from the table. I was determined to pry her out of her silence, so everyone would participate.

"Carolyn, you just finished the RP Program. How long have you been clean now?"

"I am almost up to four months, and that is the most clean time I have had in 20 years."

"How have you made it this far?"

"I look around this room and I see a whole bunch of people who care for me and want me to succeed. I never had anyone who cared about me before. If I fall down, I let them down, too. I was raised in the hood, and now I have 12 white friends at this table. I never even had 12 friends before."

The major themes seemed to be breaking out of isolation, developing a family of love and support at the Mission, discovering self-worth, and spiritual growth through praying and working together and helping others in their weaknesses. I suppose an employer sitting in his executive office might condense all of those thoughts to "developing self-esteem with the assistance of a spiritual community of support." But for those who were developing that self-esteem and who suddenly found themselves to be in a community, they called it discovering a life worth living in the most impassioned and personal words.

I realized that I didn't have to teach the seminar at all. I brought in a video camera and a tripod. I spent a few hours moving around the shop asking our workers how work at the Mission helped them as recovering addicts. They told the story themselves, so all I had to do at the convention was hit the "play" button and answer questions afterward.

CHAPTER 25

CREATIVITY

I AM CONSTANTLY AMAZED AT the talents I find among those who have become homeless. As we were going around the room with each of our homeless workers describing how Rescue Industries had helped their recoveries, Jimmy used the words, "We are the people society has thrown away and God has rebuilt."

Most of our new workers followed a very consistent pattern described by Jimmy's statement. When they first came into the shop, the only tool they felt they had mastered was the broom to sweep up the sawdust. Although on one occasion, I did have to teach proper broom technique. We had a young man who was attacking the sawdust so enthusiastically that he was sending almost as much dust into the air as he was into the piles to be scooped and bagged. I can be very patient with someone who is so excited about getting a job that he jumps in with more force than the particular task actually requires.

Scott and I were the first wood shop teachers. Then God sent a series of people, including Mr. Lopez, who had some knowledge of a useful technique that we did not know. Each new homeless teacher contributed a little more to the joint pool of knowledge. Very quickly the skill level had far surpassed anything that I had learned in high school.

As new workers come into the shop, their God-given talents start to show very quickly, and we all discover precisely where their talents can be used most effectively in the manufacturing process.

Jimmy had a gift of creative design, but he did not know it until he started working in the shop. He had never done any woodworking before coming to the Rescue Mission, nor had he ever designed anything. His addictions had control of him and had knocked him into the gutter. His family had given up on him. He had lived the experience of being thrown away. He came into the Mission with nothing, finished the 13-week RP Program, and then went to work with the other recovering addicts in the shop.

I have learned that the best potential workers to hire from the homeless population are those who have already invested thirteen weeks of their lives into coming clean. As long as we have enough furniture orders to cover the wages, I like to move our new RP graduates directly into a job at the shop so that returning to work with others from the Mission becomes the next step in the recovery process.

Scott and I had designed the first chest of drawers. I kept encouraging our workers to come up with more ideas of different products to build as well as better ways to build them, but very few of our team members brought me new ideas. I had the impression that they were afraid I would be mad at them if their idea didn't work, and they had wasted wood.

One day Jimmy came into my office and described to me what he thought would be a better method of making the corners on our chests of drawers. I listened to his idea and then told him to go build one. A week later, it was ready for my inspection.

I studied his new design and then returned to the shop at the end of the shift before our workers had gathered for closing prayer. I placed one of our old chests in the middle of the prayer circle along with the new model that Jimmy had just designed.

Once all of our workers came together for closing prayer, I announced that the older chest was built using my design, and the other one is Jimmy's design. "Look at the way Jimmy put the corners together. His design is both stronger and better looking than my design, so from now on, we will build chests the way Jimmy designed it. And Jimmy just got a raise."

Now the creativity really began to flow, and the products got better and better.

One year for Christmas, the geniuses in the shop presented me with a very special box. The sides were slightly convex and were stained darker than the top, giving it the appearance of being constructed from different types of wood. The corners were joined immaculately. The convex sides gave it an almost oval appearance that was very pleasing to the eye. On the top of the box, burned into the wood, were the words: "The Blake Barrow Executive Desk Organizer."

Most lawyers are not good organizers—hence the demand for secretaries and paralegals who have those skills. A paralegal told me that she had worked in a law office for ten years and had never seen the top of a lawyer's desk. All of the desk surfaces were covered in paper. Usually each legal case comprised a separate pile. Once I had utilized all of my desk space, the next legal pile would go to the floor around my chair. If I happened to put a case into a filing cabinet, then it stood the danger of falling into the "out-of-sight, out-of-mind" status and becoming ignored for too long.

Even though my current law practice consists of just a few *pro bono* cases being done to help Mission residents, my old lawyerly organizational system still prevails. While another lawyer would feel right at home at my desk, any organized person would view it as a disaster zone.

I opened the lid of my new Executive Desk Organizer. Inside were three red cylinders designed to imitate sticks of dynamite connected with detonation wires to a small alarm clock. My genius, homeless workers even thought to put a battery in the alarm clock so that my box was ticking down the remaining time until office reorganization.

CHAPTER 26

DOES THIS VERSION
TELL ABOUT JESUS?

A MAN WALKED UP TO the door of my office and very softly knocked on the door frame. My door was already open. I looked up at him from the work at my desk.

"Excuse me," he spoke in a very shy voice as if very reluctant to intrude. "Is it OK if I read this book?"

"Come in. Show me what you have."

He stepped into my office holding a book in his right hand. I recognized the color and texture of the book cover. It was one of the Bibles from The Gideons International that we keep on the shelf of our library.

I stepped around to the front of my desk to meet him. "Sure, you can read that book. In fact, you can have it. It's yours. We have some more."

I stuck out my right hand to greet him. "I'm Blake."

"Charlie."

"Pleased to meet you Charlie."

Up until that point, Charlie had avoided eye contact and acted like he could get in trouble if he stepped too far into the CEO's office. Then he looked at me and said, "I have heard that there are many versions of the Bible. I want to read a version that tells about Jesus. Can you tell me if this version is about Jesus?"

"Well, let me see which version that is."

He passed the book to me, and I opened it to the title page. "This is the New King James Version. That is a modern revision of the Old King James which goes all the way back to 1611. It is called the 'King James Version' because King James of England commissioned the translation. That was back around the time of Shakespeare, so the language is a bit hard for us to understand today."

About that time, I felt the Holy Spirit thump me upside the head. This man doesn't want a history lesson, he wants to learn about Jesus.

"Yes. This Bible tells the story of Jesus. Let me show you where it is." I turned to the beginning of the Gospel of Luke.

"There are four Gospels that tell the story of Jesus, and they all are right here together." I reached to my desk for a scrap of paper that he could use for a bookmark.

"Luke begins with the birth of Jesus. The next story was written by John. John began with Jesus' ministry. All four of them describe Jesus but from different sets of eyes."

I turned the pages to show him where John begins and then flipped the pages back to the bookmark and handed it to him.

"Have a seat on the couch outside my office and take your time reading. If you have any questions, I am right here."

Charlie thanked me and took his place on the couch.

I returned to my desk thinking about how I had been so thrown off guard by his bizarre question that I had fumbled such a wide open evangelical opportunity. He wanted to learn about Jesus, and I started giving him a history lesson on King James.

An hour later I saw Charlie again. He was still reading his new Bible. As inept as I felt that I had been, I was able to show him where to find the story of Jesus, and I will just let the Holy Spirit take it from there.

The encounter reminded me that you don't have to be a great theologian or an eloquent evangelist to answer his question of whether this version includes Jesus. Many of the people coming into the Rescue Mission have never heard anything about Jesus. Charlie probably had never been in a church, and he knew almost nothing about the Bible. But he had been living at the Rescue Mission for a week and had been watching our staff doing things in the name of Jesus. I was pleased that his time at the Mission had prompted him to want to read about Jesus. As inadequate as I felt I had been, eventually I got around to answering his question and showing him where to find Jesus.

CHAPTER 27

WHAT IF I WANT TO GO
VISIT MY MOTHER

OUR BOARD HAD RAISED THE issue of a major renovation
and expansion of the Rescue Mission back in 2002, but the next day
Hance McKinney called, and we went another direction since we
could buy an old, yet very solid building and fix it up at a fraction of
the cost of building a new one. No one had looked at expanding the
main building again for the next six years. Meanwhile, the condition
of our main building just got worse. When we did get some rain,
we frequently ran out of buckets trying to catch the water dripping
from the ceiling.

I felt sorry for our terminally ill guests. We had set up two
rooms for hospice care, but they were usually full, which meant that
the next person we received from a hospital would have to go into
the already overcrowded dormitory. Our mission has always been

to show the love of Jesus to those who are in great need, but the condition of the building failed to convey that message any more.

The problem was also painful in the case of women who were coming to the Mission to escape from domestic violence. Sometimes they would stay for two or three days and then return to their previous places rather than to remain in the poor living conditions presented by the women's dormitory.

A major problem was lack of money, but we got our architect to start drawing up the plans anyway. Back in 2002 we had been looking at expanding only the men's dormitory. Such a limited expansion probably would have been a mistake, as the beginning of the Great Recession was already changing the character of the homeless population coming into the Mission.

The percentage of highly educated people increased. I met a man who had been living in a suburb north of Atlanta. He had a BBA in finance and had been working as a mortgage banker. The business folded at the end of 2008. He had a house and two BMWs, but everything had a lien on it. Within three months of losing his job, both of his cars were repossessed, and two months later, his house went into foreclosure. His wife and children moved to South Carolina to live with her parents. He was from El Paso, so he came back here hoping that some of his friends could open a door for him. He confided in me with tears coming down his face that living in a homeless shelter was better than looking at his in-laws when he considered himself to be such a failure and couldn't support their daughter or his own kids.

Over the previous few years we had provided shelter for two lawyers, an engineer, a nurse, and a doctor, just to name a few. The doctor had been shot in the head, and he could not remember anything that he had learned in medical school.

The biggest change in the population was the huge numbers of women and children who were becoming homeless. The statistics from our job placement office told the whole story. In 2006 and 2007 we would place between 12 and 20 people in jobs each month. By the end of 2008, that number had dropped to one or two per month. Meanwhile, the number of men coming into the Mission had actually declined a bit. My theory was that many of the men had left El Paso for the larger cities in search of work. The numbers of broken families multiplied, and the scars caused by each broken home extended to the next generation.

Another change I noticed was that our homeless population was becoming much more disabled. Some of these people may have been able to work in prior years, but with the economic crisis, the workers with disabilities, who may not have been as productive as the others, were always the first to lose their jobs and the last to be rehired.

The changing faces of the people coming into the Mission dictated how our new floor plan needed to be drawn. We had to have a section to care for indigent patients who were being discharged by hospitals. That section also needed to be able to house people receiving hospice care. The women's side of the Mission needed to triple in size, and we needed a section designed for longer-term stays since the people who were becoming homeless were staying that way for much longer periods of time. The only way to create space for all of those needs would be to add a second floor to the building.

Toward the end of 2008 the Mission received bequests from two estates. The money was enough to bring us current on our bills and left us with enough to make a downpayment to the architect, lay the foundation, and start on the walls. The plan was that we would lay a 5,000 square-foot foundation on the side of the building and build up for two stories. Then we would have to take all the men who were living in the old men's dorm and squeeze them into the new respite care unit while we built over the top of the existing building.

Of course, most others would have gathered all of the resources they needed up front and then started construction. But my feeling was that if we published our plans in our monthly newsletter and said, "These are all of the great things we are going to build just as soon as we have $2,000,000," then we would still be waiting for the money to arrive. On the other hand, beginning construction as soon as possible would allow us to print pictures of the progress in the newsletters and show everyone that we were putting our actions behind our words. Besides, we were confident that the plan was from God, and if it was God's plan, then God would supply the resources. Our task was to step out in faith and start.

Meanwhile, I took the money that we had received from the estates and invested it in conservative stocks that still paid dividends and had recovery potential as the economy rebounded. Those investments were being made in December of 2008 and January of 2009—almost at the bottom of the market. By the time I had to cash in the stocks to pay construction costs, our investments had appreciated 150%.

The appearance of the first earthmoving machinery at the Mission brought widespread panic among our residents. At least a dozen of them asked me how long they could stay before we closed the Mission. Telling people one at a time that the Mission was not going to close did not seem to quell the unrest, so I printed up notices for a community meeting in the chapel the next day at 4:00 p.m. and posted them on the walls of the Mission. I took the architect's floor plan, taped it to a poster board, and placed it on an easel at the front of the chapel so that all of us could look at the plans together.

The community meeting was a great idea. The chapel was full, and they were all very eager to hear what I had to say. I told them of the overall plan that we were going to build around the people who were living there. Then I explained each section of the blueprints, so everyone could understand what we were building. Cheers rang out as I explained that the old men's bathroom was beyond repair and that we had to start over by building a new and much larger bath.

Before I moved to my discussion of the respite care unit on the first floor, men were asking about the new laundry room that I had drawn in next to the renovated men's dorm. There was a solid consensus that the greatest need, besides the new bathrooms, was a greatly expanded laundry room. I thought I had been so attuned to the needs of the people we were serving, yet I had failed to ask the people who were actually living in the shelter what they wanted.

Fortunately, we were still doing the basic site work and had not yet started laying the underground pipes for the plumbing, so there was still time to go back to the architect and triple the size of the laundry room.

The second floor of the new Mission would be a series of individual rooms divided into four corridors. Three of the corridors would be for single persons and the fourth, at the northwest end of the building, would provide 24 beds of transitional housing space for families. The family rooms had the bathrooms built within the rooms, so housing teenaged boys with their mothers would no longer be a problem. The individual rooms had community baths for the people within each corridor. It would look much like a college dorm, except that the rooms would be much larger than any dorm room I ever had in college.

Most of the people at the Rescue Mission had some income. Many of them were receiving social security. Since a lot of those folks wanted my help in cashing their checks, I was aware that most of the checks were between $600 and $800 per month. That amount was not enough to rent even the most economical apartment in El Paso. Sometimes those people would cash their checks and live at cheap motels for about two weeks. Then they would have to return to the Mission. Our plan was to charge $395 a month for a private room and $250 per person for a double occupancy room. That way, the price would be well within reach for a person getting a small social security check or for a person working a part-time job at minimum wage.

We designed one corridor for women and two for men since the number of our male residents was still about two-thirds of our population. I had also designed a large community room in the center of the second floor. Skylights provided natural lighting. This space would allow the people to get together outside of their rooms, and it would also provide a great space for arts and crafts for the disabled, Bible studies, and AA meetings. Since the target population for these units would be the elderly, disabled, and those who had completed our drug and alcohol program and were ready for more independent living, we would hire a new counselor to look after the residents on the second floor.

Of course, the newly renovated dormitories would still be available for people to stay without charge, but if a person wanted his or her own space, that person needed to pay for it. I have learned that people have far greater appreciation for the things they pay for.

The plan was received enthusiastically and no one complained that the price was too high.

Once I had finished explaining the proposed floor plan for the second floor, one of our guests raised his hand.

"My mother lives in Midland. If I rent one of those apartments, and I want to go visit my mother, how does that work?"

"Well," I replied, "You pack your bags. Lock your door. Tell the counselor when you will be back, and you have a nice trip."

His eyes got really big and then he exclaimed, "WOW! That's great!"

I thought we had been doing everything we could to provide hospitality for those who were staying under our roof, but his comment gave me great insight into what it was like to live in a shelter—even if it is a very nice shelter. Our dormitory was designed for people who would be there temporarily and whose possessions would fit in a backpack. We had no place to store a person's possessions securely. If someone had been able to buy a cell phone or a walkman, he would have to hide it under his mattress and hope for the best while he went to the shower.

The economy had changed the face of the homeless, but our shelter model had not changed—at least not yet. We were still set up to provide shelter for a week. Meanwhile, the changes in the economy meant that a person who became homeless may remain homeless for months or even years. Giving people the dignity of their own space where they could secure their few possessions meant everything.

I felt like I had been building what God told me to build, but I did not really know why I was building it until I heard from this man.

CHAPTER 28

HIRING STAR

I HAD HEARD JOSEPH HOBDY sing many times in church. He has a magnificent tenor voice, writes his own music, and belts it out with all the passion of an evangelist striving with every ounce of strength within him to reach one more soul for Jesus. I was thrilled when he came to me after one Sunday service and told me that he wanted to hold a concert at the church with all of the proceeds going to help the Rescue Mission.

Joseph had been watching the number of people coming into the church who had found Jesus while they were at the Mission. He also knew that our building program needed help. Construction of the new residential space had stopped until we could get more money for building materials. He had a big heart to give, but he didn't have enough money in his own pocket to buy a bucket of drywall screws. So he decided to give his time and his talents instead.

Joseph had been helping out with Celebrate Recovery, the

church's program to help people caught in addictions, so he knew who our homeless guests were. He could see beyond the scars caused by addictions and failed relationships and realized the divine potential in each person.

Of course, the Mission provided showers, clean clothes and haircuts, so we were doing a pretty good job of cleaning people up physically before they came to church.

I was sitting next to one of my friends one Sunday, and the pastor was talking about success as defined by the world and as defined by the Kingdom of God. I pulled out my church bulletin and turned to the "sermon notes" section. I jotted down a note to put in front of my pew mate:

"This morning 4 of the 8 people taking up the offering were homeless men from the Mission, and you can't tell me which ones they were. SUCCESS!"

He read the note and just smiled at me. I had twelve homeless men and women from the Mission coming with me to church that morning, and, with very few exceptions, they looked just like everyone else.

Joseph and I discussed the details of his concert for the Mission. His first question was whether we should charge a fee at the door or let everyone in free and then take an offering. I liked the offering idea. Besides, there might be some people from the Mission who would want to come but who wouldn't have $10 for admission.

About six weeks before the date set for the concert, Joseph called to set up an appointment to see me at the Mission. I could tell that he was one of those ultra-organized types who had to have every little detail planned out weeks in advance. I, on the other hand, have always been the shoot from the hip type.

Joseph came to his appointment five minutes early and brought his mother, Star, with him. I had seen Star in church, but I really didn't know her at all. She frequently assisted Joseph in church with background vocals.

Joseph started the meeting by asking me if it would be OK if he recorded our conversation. Then he set a little recorder on the edge of my desk and started asking me questions about the Mission.

After a couple of minutes, I interrupted his technique to tell him that he did not have to rehearse a speech about the work of the Rescue Mission. I was not that shy and would love to take care of the offering pitch myself. All he had to work on was the music. Joseph seemed relieved, and we continued talking about the details of the concert to come. I got even more excited when we agreed that I could dust off my bassoon and join in on a song with all of the professional musicians Joseph was bringing. Fortunately, Joseph suggested a really easy tune which I could play in the key of F. Too many sharps or flats still fluster me.

After about thirty minutes one of our workers interrupted us for a question about resuming construction on the new building. He introduced himself to Joseph and Star. I told him that Joseph sings and wants to put on a concert to benefit our construction project.

He looked at Star and asked, "And what do you do?"

"I am an intercessory prayer warrior," she replied without hesitation.

"Oh," I thought, "she must be unemployed." I don't think I had ever heard anyone respond to a question about his or her vocation in that manner.

Our meeting lasted about an hour and a half as we ironed out all of the little details. My role would come around the middle of the service. I would join in with the bassoon for three verses of "Great is Thy Faithfulness." We would invite all of the people to sing along. Then I would take the stage for a short sermon and give the sales pitch for the offering to support the new building. The professional musicians would resume with another selection as the offering was being collected.

When we had brought all of our business to a close, Star asked if she could pray for me before they left.

"Sure." I got up and walked around to the front of my desk to form a prayer circle.

Star grabbed my hand, raised her other hand into the air and started praying up a storm. Then, to my surprise, she placed her hand on my chest and started praying for the healing of my heart. The way she was praying, I knew she was talking about my physical heart and not the spiritual one.

A few months before my doctor had referred me to a cardiologist because of my high cholesterol number and the length of time that I had avoided an annual check up. The cardiologist sent me for some kind of high-tech x-ray of the heart that would show the calcium deposits within the cardiac vessels. The theory was that a plaque build-up usually contained calcium, so the test would give us a little idea of how clogged up I was. The test did come with the caution that the procedure was still experimental, so insurance would not cover any of the cost.

I paid up and took the test. A week later I got the results. I was in the 77th percentile, meaning that 77% of the men of my age had less calcium build-up than I did. Then the doctor said, "Amazingly, all of the calcium is in one vessel, and it is one of the major arteries of the heart."

At least I knew that I was not a candidate for long-term disability. The way he was describing it, I would either be here or gone—and the "gone" might come fairly quickly. I started watching my diet much more and paying up for the Lipitor, but I had told only two people about the test results, and I knew that Star could not have been in the loop to have heard of my condition.

"OK," I thought, "You really are an intercessory prayer warrior."

At least three different times during the course of our hour and a half conversation, Star had asked, "What else can I do to help the Mission?"

It was now almost 3:30 p.m. on Friday, and I had some paperwork that had to be completed before 5:00.

"There is something else that you can do for me. Go out to the wood shop, and ask for a man named Bobby. He has been having a lot of personal problems. Go pray for him just the way that you did for me."

I gave her directions to the shop and apologized for not being able to accompany her out there, but I really had to finish the paperwork and have it in the fax machine by five.

When I came in Saturday morning, I went straight to the shop to look for Bobby.

"Hey, Bobby! Did some lady come out here and pray with you yesterday?"

"Yea, man. That was awesome! It was like she knew everything I was going through without my even telling her. She was praying with me over all this stuff, and it changed my whole day. After that, I had such a sense of peace that God was taking control of all these problems, and all I had to do was quit struggling with them myself and give them to God."

Bobby's personal problems had been spilling over into his disposition on the job and the way that he was treating others.

Then it hit me. I had to hire Star as an intercessory prayer warrior for our staff. We had almost twenty workers in the wood shop who were hired from the homeless population. Of course, most of them came through our Relapse Prevention Program where they spent thirteen weeks studying the Bible, but thirteen weeks of Bible study seldom resolved the full set of personality issues that had developed over years of homelessness. Most of my problems came from employees whining to me about all of the personality conflicts they encountered in the shop. The sound was like fingernails on a chalkboard to my ears.

I imagined the scene of the next time someone came into my office complaining of another employee. I could say, "Our new policy is that before I hear about any issues that you may have with another employee, both of you are required to go pray with Star. Her office is right across the hall. If you have any unresolved issues after praying with Star, come back and see me then."

I found Star early the next week and told her that I had a job for her. She came to the Mission, and I showed her around. As we passed the kitchen, I saw a few teenagers whom I did not recognize.

"Star, we get a lot of volunteers who are ordered here by the courts to do community service. They may not know that everything we do here is for Jesus. I do not recognize any of those kids. Make sure that they know why they are here."

We continued our tour through the main building, and then I told her to go for it with the instructions to meet and pray with all of the staff and then all of the guests. About an hour later I walked by the dining room and saw Star sitting at a table with two of the teenagers that I had pointed out. She was holding a young girl's hand with one hand and had the other arm raised into the air, praying up a storm and leading both of them to Jesus.

After a couple of days, I realized that I would need to print business cards for her. The title of "Intercessory Prayer Warrior" would leave too many people shaking their heads with no understanding. Her primary job would be to pray with all of the staff and guests at the Mission. The next big problem that I had was to schedule volunteers, direct them, and equip them so that they could be more productive. Of course, all of the people wanting to volunteer also needed to know that they were coming to work for Jesus. Both tasks fit together. Then the proper title hit me: "Director of Hospitality." After all, the greatest hospitality that can ever be offered is introducing a person to Jesus.

The character of a business is revealed though its employees more than by any other factor. Why not hire a full-time person just to keep the staff and all of the guests of the Mission focused on our core values and our Christian purpose?

Within the first month of having Star on board, I know she had led at least a dozen more souls to Christ.

Star has now been on staff for over two years, and I have never heard another personality complaint by one employee against another. Everyone knows that anyone with a personality conflict must first go pray with Star, and the conflict has always resolved at that point without ever consuming any of my time.

Star is also great in keeping me focused on Jesus too. Even though my job is working for Jesus every day, those days are always divided into hundreds of smaller tasks such as making sure that we have enough food for the kitchen to prepare the next day or finding the money we need to cover payroll. It is great to be reminded of the overall focus.

As our building program started making more progress again, we got the idea to hold an open house and invite our friends to come see all the great things that their support had helped build. Preparing for an open house requires putting extra effort into cleaning the place up and having everything looking just right. We also wanted our residents to be on their best behavior as the guests who are receiving our services generally make the best tour guides.

There was one person hanging around the Mission who could have been a little problem. He claimed to be a personal friend of George Bush and kept telling me that he was going to report to "George" everything that was going on at the Mission (even though George Bush had been out of office for three years). I would try to talk to him and explain that the government had nothing to do with the running of the Mission, but he never could comprehend what I was telling him. The next day it was the same line again: "Hey, I am going to tell George what you guys are doing here."

One time he brought a lengthy hand-written letter to one of my counselors and was asking for postage to mail it to the White House. My counselor brought the letter to me asking what he should do with it. I read over the letter to make sure there were no threatening comments and then gave it back to the counselor with a postage stamp.

"Let him mail it. Maybe we can get the feds to increase funding to care for the mentally ill."

Darlene described his condition as "wet brain." I took that term to mean that he had so poisoned himself with alcohol that his brain was beyond repair.

While I wanted to care for him as best as I could, I also knew that I was wasting my time trying to give him instructions. We certainly could not have him begging money from our open house visitors or trying to talk to them about his friend George. I wanted our open house guests to get their impressions of the homeless population from the other 99.9% of the people we serve. While my view was that he was completely harmless, others without experience working with persons who are mentally ill might not perceive him that way. Yet asking him to leave was out of the question. I expressed my frustrations to Star.

Her immediate response was, "Why don't we pray and ask God who should be here for the open house?"

Of course, it was the perfectly obvious answer that I had not thought of as I was too busy running from one little problem to the next. We prayed together and gave the issue to God.

About a week before the open house, George's friend left, and I didn't see him again until after the open house.

CHAPTER 29

ORGAN KEYBOARD

MANY OF MY FRIENDS WHO regularly supported the Rescue Mission were members of a community of believers who were setting up a new church. They had purchased a building which used to be an automotive garage and were going to convert it into their new church building. I knew that they were starting with nothing but their faith and their desire to worship God, so I was praying about how to help them.

The thought occurred to me that a friend of mine who used to be on the Board of the Rescue Mission restored organs as a hobby, and then he would frequently give them to churches who were in need. He had moved to the Ft. Worth area about a year after I started working at the Mission, and I had not seen him in a few years.

I opened up my Rolodex and called Burton Patterson. He sounded pleased to hear from me and was curious about the progress at the Mission. Then I started to tell him about this new church which was converting a garage into a house of worship.

Burton interrupted me after only about three sentences of my story. "Do they sing traditional hymns?"

"Yes. They still use the old hymnals."

"Then I will give them an organ. How about a Johanus Model 25?"

"Well, I don't know what that is, but it sounds very nice."

"It is about a $20,000 organ."

"Wow, that is very generous of you."

"Well, I have learned to play only two organs at a time if I pull them close together and sit on the bench in the middle. So these extra organs need homes, but you will have to get a truck and come get it."

"No problem, I have the truck. A couple of years ago I found a 26-foot box truck with a hydraulic lift-gate for sale in a bankruptcy auction."

"That lift-gate will come in handy. This thing is really heavy."

"Let me make some other calls and study my calendar and I will call you back with when I can come."

I had ordered 40 mattresses from Peter Duncan at the Original Mattress Factory in Ft. Worth about three weeks before. I called to verify that they were ready and then told him to hold the shipping; I would come pick them up in my own truck. The organ and the mattress factory were only about 50 miles apart. I could load the organ and then pack a bunch of soft, fluffy mattresses around it for the trip home. What a great way to travel!

I blocked off three days on the calendar for the next week and called Burton back. The organ was at the home of a lady who had been playing for their church. Since she had decided to concentrate on the piano, this organ was getting little use. If I left work around 3:00 p.m. one afternoon, I could spend the night in a motel along the way and be at the house with the organ before noon the next day.

When I reached the house, I was very relieved to discover that Burton had recruited a half-dozen members of the high school football team who had just finished one of their summer morning practices.

Burton fired up the organ and played a few hymns. What a magnificent sound!

I had brought a collection of hand-trucks and 4-wheel dollies from El Paso, so we were able to roll the organ to the truck once we got it out to the front porch. I was very thankful for the football team. It took three of us just to lift up one end so that a dolly could slide under it.

Once it was in the driveway, all of the hard work was done. We rolled it onto the lift-gate and then into the truck where I strapped it to the side of the truck. I closed up the back of the truck and was ready to roll.

Burton suggested that I follow him to the local Subway where he paid the football team by buying them all of the food they could eat.

Within another two hours, I was at the mattress factory loading up. The factory workers would pile the mattresses on the lift-gate, and I would carry them to the front of the truck so that everything was packed tightly.

Peter came out to see me after we had loaded about half the order.

"Hey, I have an idea. I have 35 mattresses that need to go to the rescue mission in Las Cruces. That is right up the road from you, isn't it?"

"Only 35 miles away."

"I'll give you some diesel money to take them up there."

"Sure, let's see if it will all fit."

I had placed the mattresses in the truck standing on their ends. Each one was 75 inches long, so that left some room between the mattresses and the roof of the truck. I took some of the mattresses I had placed on their ends and shoved them on the top to fill all of the available space. I could fit three more mattresses between my row of vertical mattresses and the ceiling of the truck.

I finished loading all of my mattresses and then the Las Cruces order started coming. These were different. All of them were standard twin size like the ones I had ordered, but mine were foam whereas the Las Cruces mattresses were built around metal wire frames with springs in the middle. Those were three times as heavy, and the wire frames made for very rigid edges. I took a couple of my pliable, foam mattresses and placed them in front of the organ so that none of the rigid edges would rub against its finish, and then I continued loading the other order and stacking mattresses all the way to the ceiling.

The fit was amazing, if not miraculous. Every mattress from both orders was in the back of the truck, but there was not room for even one more.

I was back in El Paso the following evening, but the first thing off the truck had to be the Las Cruces order since it was stacked in the rear. The next morning I checked my messages, made sure everything was going well at the Mission, and then called Las Cruces to let them know that I would be there with mattresses in another forty-five minutes.

Unloading things at rescue missions is always quick and easy. They announced that unloading labor was needed, and within a few minutes, I had twenty helpers. I raised the back door, climbed in, and started passing mattresses down to waiting hands. After about five minutes of unloading, I was already back to the position of the organ. I took a moment to appreciate the beauty of its finish. It was in perfect condition and had not moved a fraction of an inch since we loaded it.

The first mattresses that had to come off the next row were those that were stuffed near the ceiling. Then I could pull out the mattresses that were standing on their ends on the floor of the truck.

I reached up as high as I could, grabbed a mattress, and started pulling it back from the stack. As I pulled back, I saw the mattress above it starting to slide over the top of the mattress I was holding. It slid off of the stack and landed behind me with a strange thump. I brought the other mattress down and then turned to see that the upper mattress had crashed directly into the organ's keyboard. Apparently, the metal frame of that mattress landed squarely on one of the keys and fractured it into five or six pieces. The largest piece was lying on the floor of the truck. Other fragments were in the keyboard. The largest section was about half the size of my thumb, but other slivers were barely wider than a toothpick.

The keyboard reminded me of an old "Dennis the Menace" show when Dennis had just lost one of his incisors and there was a big, dark hole in the front of his smile. My stomach cramped up in knots, and I felt like throwing up. What had I done?

I got the rest of the Las Cruces mattresses off the truck and then scoured the area for more pieces. The white key had broken off next to the tip of the adjacent black key. I could see more little parts down in the keyboard, but I would need a pair of tweezers to fish them out.

I drove back to El Paso kicking myself all the way for ever attempting to transport those mattresses. I knew that I had only myself to blame as I had both loaded and unloaded the truck. I could have laid one of our foam mattresses on top of the organ as well, but I didn't do it.

I stopped at the Walgreens on the way into El Paso for a tube of superglue. It was worth a try.

I spent the next hour at my desk trying to place each splinter in the right position and then giving it a fine bead of superglue before proceeding to the next part. I soon discovered that I didn't have all the parts. Furthermore, the glue residue was getting on the top of the key so that it was impossible to regain the original, smooth finish.

Who was I trying to kid? I had destroyed the key, and it was beyond my ability to fix it. I needed professional help.

My first thought was to call Kenny Capshaw. He played in the El Paso Symphony and had his own music store. I grabbed the phone book, but he was not listed. I tried putting his name into Google, and I still found no phone number, but it did provide a link to the El Paso Conservatory of Music.

I called them and told the person answering the phone that I had a crisis with an organ and needed to find Kenny Capshaw. He told me that he could pass a message to Mr. Capshaw but that he was not permitted to give out his number. Then he said, "I play the piano. Maybe I can help you. What is the problem."

I told him how I had knocked out a key with a mattress frame and the keyboard looked like a kid who had just lost an incisor.

"What kind of organ is it?"

"A Johannus Model 25."

"Oh, well there is nobody in El Paso who could help you with that. Johannus organs are very rare, and they don't share any parts with any other brands. But I know what you can do. The expert on organs like that is Burton Patterson. Have you tried calling him?"

"NO! Burton gave me the organ just two days ago. It is a gift for a church here in El Paso. I can't tell him that I have destroyed his organ!"

"Oh man, you really are in trouble."

After a few seconds of further agony, he said, "The last I heard, there was a Johannus dealer in the Austin area, and I believe he is the only dealer in the state of Texas. Try looking him up and see if he is still there."

I thanked him for his assistance and pulled up the Google screen again. Indeed, I did find a listing for Johannus of Texas and a phone number. By this time it was close to four o'clock in El Paso, which meant that it was almost five in Austin. I called the number, but no one answered, and the call went to an answering machine. I left a message and then tried to occupy myself with something else.

About two hours later my cell phone rang. I glanced at the number before answering. It was from the (512) area code which is Austin! It was the Johannus man calling me back.

I explained what I had done.

"What model is it?"

"A Model 25."

"Nope, there is no such thing."

"How many keyboards does it have? Two or three?"

"Let me think…I believe it is two. All I could really remember was that big black hole in what was supposed to be white. I wasn't thinking about the number of rows."

He asked me a few more questions that I was unable to answer and then said, "Well, all of these keyboards are different."

"OK, I see that I am going to have to get you to examine this organ." My mind started racing ahead to how quickly I could drive the big truck to Austin. "Do you ever come to El Paso?"

"As a matter of fact, I am in El Paso right now. I just finished installing an organ at the Jesus and Mary Catholic Church. Do you know where that is?"   .

"THE JESUS AND MARY CHURCH! You are less than a thousand yards from the organ! The street in front of the church is Yandell. Take the Yandell bridge over the Interstate, and the first street on the right is the entrance to the Rescue Mission. You will see a big box truck in the driveway. The organ is inside the truck. I am about five miles away right now, so you will get there before I will, but just wait right there."

I hung up the phone and raced back to the Mission. Sure enough, there was a delivery van in the driveway behind my truck with "Johannus of Texas" written on its side. I rushed over to greet these angels from heaven and then opened the back of the truck for them.

We stepped into the truck and looked at the keyboard. "I think I have most of the parts. I started glueing them back together."

He chuckled a bit at my efforts and went back to his van for a few tools.

Within five minutes he had the back of the organ removed and the keyboard lifted out of the main body.

"I am pretty sure I have one of these keys back in my shop. Now watch how I am going to remove this broken key, and you just follow the same procedure in reverse to put a new key on. I'll just put the key in the mail to you. Send me a check for $25—that will cover the key and postage."

The knots in my stomach were gone. For the first time all day I felt a tremendous sense of relaxed relief.

As I was driving home thinking about the day's events, suddenly I started to laugh. "OK, God. I get it. I destroyed this man's $20,000 organ while trying to do your work in helping a church and in helping another mission. Meanwhile, the only person in the whole state of Texas, other than Burton Patterson, who could fix it was working a few blocks away. I got it. You are in control, and all I have to do is keep my eyes on you. I may mess up, but you will fix it."

The key came in the mail a few days later, and I remembered how to take the organ apart and install the new key. I gladly mailed in a check for $25. If only the tuition for all divine lessons were that cheap!

CHAPTER 30

ENTITLEMENT

I WAS WORKING AT MY desk about nine in the morning when two men walked through the open door. The first man did all the talking.

"We need new shirts."

"Yes sir, I see that you do."

Both of their shirts were soiled as if the men had been camping out for a week without a fresh change. The dirt was nothing that a half cup of Tide could not conquer, but they probably had nothing else to wear while their shirts were washing.

"We keep our clothing in the old grain silo at the end of the property. George runs the clothing distribution. He usually opens up around 9:30 or 10:00, but you can check at the front desk to be sure."

"Look, we have things to do. We can't wait around for whoever George is. We want our shirts now."

"I am sorry. I don't even have the key. You will have to wait for George."

Then he produced one of the most brilliant lines of logic that I have ever heard.

"The people of El Paso gave you that clothing so that you can give it to us, didn't they?"

"Yes, that is true."

"So you have my shirt, and I want my shirt now!"

I had to break out in a big grin at his reasoning.

"I am sorry. I cannot help you."

They turned and left, and I never saw them again. I don't know if they ever got new shirts. Fortunately, I have found such a "you owe me" attitude to be rare among the people we serve, but whenever I see it, I turn them away without regret and with a quick, "I'm sorry. I can't help you." Such a person is incapable of really being helped.

Any able-bodied person who has such a brilliant grasp of logic should have no trouble finding a job.

CHAPTER 31

COMMUNITY OF FAITH FIFTH GRADE

A FIFTH-GRADE TEACHER FROM THE Community of Faith School called me about scheduling a tour of the Rescue Mission for her class. She wanted to make sure that I would be the one directing the tour, and then she wanted her students to participate in serving lunch. The more I talked with the teacher, the more of a sense I had that she was looking for a real hands-on experience rather than an informational visit.

I prayed about what form the visit should take and then got an idea. If the class wanted to know who the people were who were living at the Rescue Mission, they should have the opportunity to talk with our guests themselves. To make that task a little easier for them, I would draw up a survey of questions so that each kid could ask open-ended questions and take notes of their answers.

The top of the survey had an introductory line: "Hi, my name is
_____. I go to the Community of Faith School, and I am
taking a survey for the Mission that will help the Mission provide
better service. May I sit down and speak with you?"

The survey then began with a few easy questions that would not
be too personal in order to start a conversation: "What has been your
favorite meal since coming to the Rescue Mission?"

"What was the best part about that meal?"

"How long have you been at the Mission?"

"How long have you been homeless?"

"What has the Mission provided to you that was the most
helpful?"

"What else do you think the Mission could do that would be
helpful to you?"

Then I stuck in a few questions that would get both of them
thinking:

"Describe to me what your life was like when you were my age."

"When you were my age, what did you want to be when you
grew up?"

"What do you think you will be doing five years from now?"

The last line was, "Tell me what you think caused you to become
homeless."

I printed up enough copies of the survey so that each child could get
two, and then I waited with great anticipation for the date of this
experiment which I had never tried before.

The school bus pulled up to the front of the Mission around
11:00 a.m., and we directed the class of twenty kids into the chapel.
I introduced myself and told them a little about the Rescue Mission,
but I was careful not to say too much about the mixture of people
who were living with us.

After about a five-minute introduction, I said, "Now, I want feedback from you. Who do you think these people are who are living here at the Rescue Mission?"

No immediate response, so I rephrased the question: "Why do you think these folks are homeless?"

That question got a reluctant hand into the air.

"They don't have jobs."

"Good answer! The unemployment rate in El Paso is typically one of the highest in the state of Texas. We have a lot of people who want jobs, but they are unable to find work."

"What else?"

My encouraging reply to the first brave kid got several more hands into the air, and the list of potential causes kept growing.

"Drugs."

"Yes, that is a big one, although it's not as big of a category as some people might think. Roughly one-third of the people coming into the Mission struggle with drug or alcohol addictions."

"Unstable families."

I was impressed with the way the kid phrased it. "Is this a sixth grade class?"

"No, fifth."

"Wow, you guys are smart. Yes, I think broken families may be the number one category in causing homelessness—particularly if you consider the effects that broken families have on the children. In fact, a very substantial number of homeless people in America are children just like yourselves."

One boy raised his hand and said, "They smoke."

"Interesting, out of all the groups of children or adults that I have shown around the Mission, I have never had anyone identify smoking as a cause of homelessness, but you are absolutely correct! In fact, I will do an exercise for the people enrolled in our Relapse Prevention Program. I ask them how much does a pack of cigarettes cost? Then I write the number on the board. How many packs do you smoke in a week? Usually the numbers presented to me are between five and ten. I will take the average of those numbers and multiply the average by the cost of one pack. Then I multiply the weekly total by 52. Their eyes usually get real big, and they are amazed at the fact that they are spending close to $3000 a year burning tobacco."

"Other than spending all of that money on cigarettes, how can smoking lead to homelessness?"

"It causes health problems."

"Very good! And health problems create medical bills and reduce your performance at work."

The ideas just kept coming for about twenty minutes. Once all of their ideas had been presented, I told them of the exercise I had planned.

"OK, now that you have given me your ideas about who the people are who are at the Rescue Mission and why they are homeless, we are going to take some time and talk to some of our residents directly."

I got the teacher to pass out two surveys per child, and then we passed around a box of pencils. We practiced the introduction together and went through the rest of the survey questions.

"Now, it is almost lunch time. Our guests will file through the dining room, get a tray of food, and sit down at a table to eat. Your job is to find someone who has an empty spot at the table, sit down with them, and strike up a conversation. These survey questions are just a tool to allow you to get the information that you are looking for. Every student must do two interviews. If you can't find anyone at a table with a vacant seat, go to the back porch, and you will find more people sitting on the benches in the back. Once you have interviewed two people, you may get your own lunch tray and sit down to eat. When everyone has taken two surveys and eaten lunch, come back into the chapel and have a seat."

"Any questions?"

They all seemed to get it on the first explanation. I looked to the back of the room at their teacher who had a slightly cautious smile on her face. I had not warned her or my homeless residents of my experiment.

We announce the opening of the lunch line over the Mission's intercom. The announcement had come five minutes before, so I knew there would be people already sitting at tables in the dining room.

"OK, let's hit it. The dining room is right across the hall. We meet back here after lunch."

Within about forty-five minutes all of the kids were back in the chapel. This time the noise level was quite elevated as they were busy comparing notes.

"OK," I shouted, "everybody take a seat."

"Now that you have had a chance to talk with some of our guests, let me ask you the same question that we started with. Who are these folks who are living at the Rescue Mission?"

A boy in the first row shot his hand enthusiastically into the air. "They are people just like me."

"YES! YES! THAT'S IT! You got the lesson!"

Other students wanted to share their experiences, too. "One lady told me that I reminded her of her daughter that she has not seen in ten years, then she told me what a blessing I had been by talking to her."

No one had encountered a homeless guest who did not want to talk.

After ten minutes of sharing, it was time to reload the bus. As I walked out with the group, their teacher told me that her call had been prompted by a disparaging comment that one of her students had made about a person who was homeless. The exercise had been perfect.

CHAPTER 32

MY FRIEND

BRIAN, ONE OF OUR CHEFS, was moving from a small apartment to his own home, and he wanted my help with our big truck for the move. He had scheduled Sunday afternoon as moving time.

I had driven the truck to Houston to deliver a load of bunk beds from our shop to the Mission of Yahweh, a shelter for women and children, and I was planning to be back in El Paso by around 3:00 p.m., but I had gotten a late start to the day. After unloading the truck Saturday morning, helping carry things into their shelter, and showing their workers how to put the beds together, I was pretty tired and slept late. Then I discovered that the cafe next to my motel in Junction served an outstanding chili and cheese omelet, and the time spent savoring it simply could not be rushed. I didn't pull into El Paso until close to 5:00 p.m.

I got to Brian's apartment about sunset and was a little surprised to see all of his things placed by the curb at the bottom of the stairs.

What a pile it was! It was a good thing the truck was completely empty after the Houston delivery. We started loading in the most space-efficient means possible. The truck box is 26 feet long and eight feet wide. When the last item was finally shoved in, only one foot of space remained to pull down the door.

Fortunately, Brian had recruited a helper—a man from the Mission named Thomas. Brian and Thomas had carried all of Brian's things down the stairs from his second floor apartment, and the three of us loaded the truck. Thomas was almost 60 years old and not in the best of health, but he kept moving things into the truck as quickly as Brian was.

Once the last of Brian's belongings had been moved from the curb to the truck, Brian and Thomas got into Brian's car, and I followed them in the truck to Brian's new home.

Unloading always seems easier than loading. The end of the task is in view, and there is no concern for things being placed just right so that they don't fall and break with the movement of the truck. Also, Brian was so grateful for the trucking assistance that he didn't ask for help moving anything inside his new home.

"Just get it off the truck and onto the curb, and I will do the rest."

Since it was already about 8:00 p.m. and I had covered 440 miles in the truck earlier in the day, I didn't insist on providing further moving assistance.

As I pulled away, Brian and Thomas were carrying a large couch into Brian's new home. Monday was Brian's scheduled day off, and I am sure he spent the whole day arranging all his stuff.

Brian was back in the kitchen early Tuesday morning. He thanked me for the trucking assistance and then told me the rest of the story. Thomas had stayed with Brian from 2:00 that afternoon until 10:30 that night helping to move all of his furniture out of the old apartment, onto the truck, and then into the new house.

When everything was off the curb and into the house, Thomas said, "Do you know why I am helping you?"

"No," Brian replied. "I am just glad that you are."

"Last week you were showing your wife around the Mission, and you stopped and introduced me to her. You said, 'This is my friend, Thomas.' No one has ever introduced me as his friend."

CHAPTER 33

I WANT TO DO WHAT
YOU ARE DOING

I WAS WALKING INTO CHURCH one Sunday morning
when I saw my good friend Dr. Russell van Norman. If you could
imagine who Dr. Marcus Welby would be if taken off the screen and
put into real life, that person would come close to Dr. van Norman.
He lived a simple life of humility and service to others, doing all he
could to better the health of everyone in the community. Rather than
to be a part of a more financially lucrative practice, he preferred to
work in the county hospital where he could serve people's health
needs without having to be concerned about business practices.

To my astonishment, he told me that he had just retired.

"Retired! You are too young for that!"

"Well, I just turned 65."

Russell looked like he wasn't even 60.

"What are you going to do now?"

"I want to do what you are doing," Russell replied. "I want to go to the mission field and preach the Gospel while using my medical knowledge to help others."

In less than a week I got the news that Russell was dead. He stepped off a curb to cross a street when he was hit by a car that didn't stop.

I have wondered how long Russell had felt a calling to the ministry before he finally answered that call. I had the feeling from our conversation that God had been tugging on his heart for some time, but when he finally answered, his time was up, and he never got to go.

I am so thankful that God called me to ministry at the Rescue Mission at the age of only 39. I was approaching the prime time of my legal career, but the law practice offered no sense of fulfillment close to what I have experienced in proclaiming the Gospel of Jesus to the poor. I thought I was perfectly happy trying lawsuits until I experienced something far better.

I have described my calling to some of my friends whom I knew were financially well established. They would look at me with envy and say, "I would love to do what you are doing, but my kids are still in college," or they would give an abundance of other excuses as to why they needed to concentrate on their businesses and make more money. My kids had not yet started college at the time I joined the Mission. Somehow God provided, and all of their tuition and other college expenses were paid.

Many of you who have read this book are feeling God's call on your life. It is a call to serve God with your whole life, and the major part of your life is your job. Please do not delay. Answer the call and give your whole life to Jesus right now. You will discover that God's presence, power, and blessings follow your obedience, "and my God will meet all your needs according to the riches of his glory in Christ Jesus." (Phil. 4:19 *NIV*)

EPILOGUE

by
TAYLOR HERNANDEZ

I COME FROM A WELL-OFF family with parents of two different religions and three siblings with three different perceptions of who God is. I went to a Jewish Academy until I was five years old and then to a Christian School from Kindergarten to 8th grade. We lit the menorah the eight nights of Hanukkah, made Hamantaschen at Purim, yet celebrated Jesus on Christmas and Easter. My parents ensured we would have the chance to experience these two altering religions and decide for ourselves whom we wanted to be. The gift of hearing stories from the Bible throughout nine years at St. Clement's School was, without a doubt, the greatest gift I could ever receive. I thought I had found God. I prayed every night to praise God, thanked Him for all that I had, for the forgiveness of my sins, for others and their well being, and lastly for myself to be the best person I could be. However, it was not until I was introduced to the Rescue Mission of El Paso that I realized the hidden meaning behind the prayers.

Our school assigned us a project to gather items to donate to the Mission and then to serve food and spend an afternoon with people who were living at the Mission. After months of acquiring these items through several canned food drives, clothing and toiletries collections, our 8th grade class went over to the Rescue Mission and set up several tables of items to give to the people staying there.

Smiles.

I had never seen so many smiles.

When the bristles on my toothbrush are worn, I look underneath my sink to find two new toothbrushes available. Once those run out, I walk downstairs to our laundry room to find ten other new toothbrushes.

"Mom, my shampoo makes my hair greasy. Can you get me another one?"

"No, Mom! This shampoo dries out my hair like crazy! Get me another one!"

Never had I ever realized the value of an item as simple as a toothbrush before my experience at the Rescue Mission. Each and every person there was thankful. My peers and I were giving away our old clothes, blankets that we told our moms to buy us to donate, old towels, and bathroom essentials—items kids like us never thought would not be readily available. It was a task as easy as giving away "stuff" we didn't want, yet the difference, although small at first, was tremendous. That night it occurred to me that I wanted to make a difference larger than a material offering. I wanted to change the lives of the people at the Mission and help them in any way I could. Little did I know then that they would be the ones who would have such an impact on my life.

Entering high school I was aware that I would need to become active in some sort of volunteer work, but let's be honest. I was fifteen years old, that stuff is a drag, and quite frankly, my mom was the one making me do it. I told her that the Rescue Mission would be the most fun because I remembered enjoying it the previous year. My mom agreed and my journey began.

I walked into Blake's office anxious to see the passionate man I was introduced to before. He told me I would be working in their wood shop with a woman named Jamie. The items made in the wood shop would be sold to churches all over Texas, and the work provided job opportunities for several unemployed, homeless people living there.

Jamie taught me how to make one of their most popular items, a mesquite wood cross. She had already cut several crosses, and we would carve out the cracks to amplify the unevenness. We crushed turquoise and used it to fill in the crevices to make the cross even. Then we topped it with an epoxy. No two crosses were alike, each with their own design. She was much better at it than I was, and I hoped I wasn't doing anything wrong.

The day was coming to a close, and I wanted to say goodbye to Blake before I left. I peeked in his office, smiled and told him I would see him tomorrow. As I turned my head I noticed several crosses similar to the ones I had made that afternoon. Upon each was a tag that read, "...The mesquite wood is cut from trees which grow in very arid areas of south Texas. The dry climate causes the interior of the trees to crack. Our homeless workers have cleaned out the cracks and filled them with crushed turquoise and epoxy before applying a smooth finish. We have some similarities with the wood. We all have our cracks too, but when we allow God to clean and fill our cracks, then our cracks become our most beautiful parts...." Naturally, I was touched.

The following day I expected a quick hello and a busy day in the wood shop when Blake asked me to take a seat. He asked what

I thought of Jamie and the Mission itself. He then went on to tell me about the homeless people who were living there.

First thing's first—people's conception of the "homeless" has GOT to be the BIGGEST misconception in the history of misconceptions.

Like most people, I was under the impression that these people threw away their lives, didn't care, and didn't want to make a change. My siblings and I have it all, but that doesn't mean we are going to rely on our trust funds and parents' hard work to get places in life. As cliché as it sounds, we are all equal, and we all have the chance to do something magnificent, so why should I feel obligated to help these people? Life is about choices, and every decision we make either has a positive or negative consequence, but the beauty of it is that we have the ability to control the outcome. I found it difficult to sympathize with people who didn't work to make a change in their lives and let them crumble to pieces. It was after Blake talked to me that I realized how wrong I was.

He told me the story about Tammy, whose older brother shot her with heroin when she was only nine years old. I asked myself how it was possible that anyone could pursue a healthy life after that.

There was a lawyer who graduated at the top of his class and worked with a great firm after graduating and specializing in trial law. He was haunted by every question he forgot to ask in court, every sentence he could have phrased differently, and any slight piece of evidence he failed to mention. He struggled to communicate at the level of the jury and didn't know how to appeal to them. Consequently, he lost a series of cases, and all the remaining jobs he had were more steps down the ladder. Once Blake found him and realized this man could excel in a different type of law, such as writing contracts, he was already in the process of being disbarred.

He had no job, no income, and nowhere to go—an intelligent lawyer, homeless.

In that moment it occurred to me that the people living at the Mission were no different from my siblings, my friends, or myself. We never know, and will never be prepared for, what life is going to throw at us and what bumps we will hit on the road.

The rest of the summer I took the time to learn Jamie's story, and it humbled me. The difficulties and plights she faced were beyond my imagination. My perspective on life had changed. I realized it wasn't about how many times you go to church in a week, how many stories of the Bible you have memorized, how many icons you wear around your neck, or how much money you are able to donate, but about being the person you want to meet.

I admired Blake's zealousness. His passion was electrifying. He opened my eyes to the joys of doing something for someone other than myself. He taught me the significance of putting someone else's needs in front of my own. I became a better person. I was definitely more appreciative, and I learned the difference between desires and necessities. My parents were happy to see I was not as cranky around the house, and I embraced each day in a new way. I became extremely active in clubs at school to ensure the well-being of the student body, which was a great way to kick off my freshman year in high school. Education became a gift, and I did not want to take a single class for granted. As a result, I'm the valedictorian of the Class of 2015 (Let's hope that stays). Life became a world filled with infinite possibilities that I was exhilarated to experience each and every day. Most profoundly, I became a great listener, and I found my own peace and self-satisfaction in going the extra mile to help out a friend, pay for a stranger in line at lunch, take the time to stop someone from bullying another, clean the leftover lunch scraps after a meeting, and basically anything to make someone's day that much better.

The Bible verses, the sermons, the prayers—they finally made sense, they had a purpose. It's as simple as smiling, learning to dance in the rain, helping those in need, loving your enemies, and learning day by day to make the Lord, our God, happy.

I have been volunteering at the Rescue Mission of El Paso for four years and counting. It's no longer a chore; it's a chance to make a difference.